The

Essence of Faith

According to Luther

The
Essence of Faith
According to Luther

LUDWIG FEUERBACH

Translated by Melvin Cherno
(DEPARTMENT OF HISTORY, OAKLAND UNIVERSITY,
ROCHESTER, MICHIGAN)

Harper & Row, Publishers
NEW YORK, EVANSTON, AND LONDON

THE LIBRARY OF RELIGION AND CULTURE
GENERAL EDITOR: *Benjamin Nelson*

Contents

Introduction

I. LUDWIG FEUERBACH IN 1844

The year 1844 was a busy one in the life of the German philosopher Ludwig Feuerbach (1804–1872). The former student of theology and of Hegelian philosophy had during the previous decade attained the insight that a frontal attack against both Hegelianism and orthodox religion was a necessary prerequisite for an enlightened political, social, and economic order. In 1841 he had burst before the reading public with his remarkable study, *The Essence of Christianity*, a work which shocked half its readers, stimulated the other half, and was received by both groups as no work had been received since Hegel's writings decades before.

In 1842 and 1843 he had clarified in his own mind,

and published in a pair of brief essays, the foundations
of a new philosophy of "sensualism" (*Sinnlichkeit*);
one, that is, which stressed individualized human existence as the basis for all political and social theory.
By 1844 Feuerbach had published a revised edition of
The Essence of Christianity, and now found himself
praised or condemned from all sides as the leader of
an anti-Hegelian and antitheological revolt. It was in
1844 that his publisher prevailed upon him to prepare
revised editions of some of his historical and critical
works and, in the spring, both publisher and philosopher began to give serious thought to a complete
edition of all his writings, a project which was to be-
gin within two years and which would end only with
the publication of the tenth volume of *Complete
Works* two decades later.

The year 1844 was significant for personal reasons,
too. Feuerbach spent the summer acquainting himself with radical social theorists—Wilhelm Weitling,
primarily, whose *Guarantees of Freedom and Har-
mony* especially impressed him. Before the end of the
year a tragedy had also taken place—he had lost his
daughter and, like Cicero, attempted, not successfully,
to temper his distress with philosophic sobriety. At
the same time, his study of Christianity continued; it
was the writings of Martin Luther that occupied most
of his attention. It was in the early part of this event-
ful year that he published the essay with which we are
concerned, *The Essence of Faith According to*

Luther (*Das Wesen des Glaubens im Sinne Luthers*), usually referred to by the author simply as *Luther*.

II. THE LUTHER ESSAY—ITS PLACE IN FEUERBACH'S WORKS

If any of Feuerbach's works is convenient as a central point for the study of his thought, it is the essay of 1844 entitled *The Essence of Faith According to Luther*. Written as a kind of supplement to *The Essence of Christianity*, it nevertheless goes beyond that work in some important respects, and clearly foreshadows the later stages of Feuerbach's religious investigations as well. Furthermore, it is an excellent example of the style and method of most of his other works and indicates his major strengths and weaknesses as a writer.

A word first about the general development of Feuerbach's views on religion. His great aim was to indicate that man, not God, was the creator, and that divinities were representations of man's innermost feelings and ideas. His first conception was represented by *The Essence of Christianity*. In this work, Feuerbach saw God as the result of man's abstraction from the characteristics of human nature—particularly the characteristics of the human race as a whole—and the subsequent establishment of this abstraction as a real entity. Men looked about them, saw that their ideals of perfection were not realized in particular human beings, and, supposing that these ideals must

be realized in some being, created a God; in doing
this they overlooked the fact that the locus of these
ideals—justice, truth, love—was indeed apart from
individual human beings, but was in the human race as
a whole, not in a superhuman divinity. In the second
stage, represented by *The Essence of Religion*
(1845), a brief work, and the much fuller *Lectures
on the Essence of Religion* which he delivered in
Heidelberg in 1848–1849 as his contribution to the
revolutionary activity of that year, Feuerbach broad-
ened his field to include non-Christian religions. He
now saw Christianity and other *Geistesreligionen* as a
later stage of religious development, being preceded
by a period of *Naturreligionen*, nature worship. In the
former the divinity was derived from human characteristics; the latter based divinity upon objects in the
world around man, inanimate and animate alike. The
generalization developed to cover both these cases was
that religion derived from man's feeling of dependence—in the early stages, dependence upon nature;
later, as civilized arts developed and nature's power
over men lessened, upon men. In any case, men feared,
were grateful to, and worshiped those beings upon
which they felt their existence depended. As Feuerbach probed the psychological bases of religious behavior, he developed a hypothesis he felt was still
more adequate to explain the various facets of religious
development. In the *Theogonie* (1857), for example,
he pointed out that both man's awareness of his ideals
and his awareness of dependence on other beings

could be brought together as aspects of a kind of
generalized urge toward happiness. According to this
view man always assumed that his desires were obtain-
able. To validate this assumption, men looked to their
gods as the fulfillers, guarantors, or representatives of
human wishes. The origin of gods thus lay not in a
negative dependence on nature and men, but in a positive drive which assumed that human wishes were in
accord with the nature of the world.

The Essence of Faith According to Luther provided a transition between the first two stages. *The
Essence of Christianity* had attempted to establish that
the Christian God was simply an abstraction made up
of concepts dear to the heart of man; what man desired desperately on earth, he created for himself in
heaven, giving to God all those characteristics he
wished for himself. The new essay was an attempt to
provide documentary evidence for the truth of this
generalization. Through statements by Martin Luther,
Feuerbach attempted to show that all religious notions had man's welfare as an ultimate goal. Following
The Essence of Christianity, he wanted to make the
point that what Christians called "faith" was simply
the certainty that God was primarily a man-oriented
being. In a sense, then, *The Essence of Faith According to Luther* was only an attempt to put into a more
concrete form the main ideas of the earlier work—
concrete in the sense that he could find specific statements by Luther to back up his generalizations. It is
more than likely that the direct stimulus to the writ-

ing of the essay was a passage in the very last paragraphs of the appendix of *The Essence of Christianity*,
in which Feuerbach characterized the entire Reforma-
tion movement as having overthrown the older
Catholic unconcern for the corporeal existence of
men and as having stressed the human orientation of
God.

The relation of the two works is close in another
sense also. Feuerbach, despite his opposition to the
implications of theology which he felt dangerous to
human welfare, always indicated a remarkable sympathy for the religious point of view. The very or-
ganization of *The Essence of Christianity* is significant in this regard. The book was divided into two
parts which treated, respectively, the "true" and the
"false" aspects of theology. The "truth" of religion
was the fact that in religion man expressed his most
intimate thoughts and ideas; the "falsity" of religion
consisted of man's distortion of these thoughts and
ideas by considering them attributes of a superhuman
and supernatural being. This concept runs all the way
through Feuerbach's religious analyses; always he saw
a false façade overlying the essentially valid and valuable conception. It was this façade which had to be
rejected, just as it was the true basis of religion which
had to be purified and seen in its proper light, or
"brought down to earth." In *The Essence of Christianity*, for example, the "truth" of religion lay in the
validity of the various ideals which men worshiped as
"God"; the "falsity" of religion lay in the establish-

ment of this "God" as a collective name for a group of ideals which in reality were to be found in *human* conduct and behavior. In the first part of the work, he attempted to "explain" the human ideals and desires behind the various conceptions of Christianity; in the second part, to indicate the incongruity of establishing a God in order to recognize these ideals. His attitude toward religion, in short, was ambivalent; he admired and tried to uphold its truth, at the same time attempting to destroy its falsity. His attitude toward Luther betrayed the same ambivalence. He admired Luther because of Luther's ultimate aim—the welfare of man; but he execrated Luther for failing to recognize that love toward humanity should be exercised directly—that is, by worshiping man, not God. This it was which could lead Feuerbach to make the following statement:

> Is the work *The Essence of Faith According to Luther* for or against Luther? It is just as much for as against Luther. But is this not a contradiction? Certainly; but a necessary contradiction, rooted in the nature of the object itself.

By 1844 Feuerbach had become aware of an inconsistency in his previous thought. In his philosophical writings of 1842 and 1843, he had attacked the Hegelian tendency toward overabstraction. As a matter of fact, he felt that Hegelianism was simply another form of theology, in that the Hegelian Absolute was formed in the same way as the Christian God:

from human characteristics considered in the abstract and reified into a hypothetical being. But his attack against abstraction was not complete; he had himself taken the position that the human species should be the object of man's respect and worship. This, actually, was one of the principal criticisms made against Feuerbach by Marx and Engels—the fact that he never (according to them) saw the abstractness of his own concept of the "species." In reality, Marx and Engels were wrong. Feuerbach did recognize that the "race" was too idealistic a conception for a philosopher whose primary concern was individualized, concrete, sensual human existence. It was his recognition of this principle of "sensualism" (*Sinnlichkeit*)—the view that priority must be given to the individual sentient being—that he later referred to as his "shaking off" of the last remnants of idealism. And he felt that this had occurred in the Luther essay. The following passage is from the foreword to the first volume of *Complete Works*, written in 1846:

You [the philosopher is speaking to himself] recognized that the being which, as a being of a different nature, is set off from sensual beings, is itself nothing but the abstract or idealized essence of sensuality. This insight you gained first in the field of religion. . . . But what you recognized as the essential characteristic of religion was not at first the most essential thing for you, for your consciousness, or for your understanding, at least theoretically.

You were still haunted by the abstract Rational Being, the being of philosophy, as distinct from the actual, sensual being of nature and humanity. Your *Essence of Christianity* was, at least partially, written when you still looked at things in this contradictory manner. Only in your *Luther*—which thus is by no means a mere "supplement," as the title says, but had independent significance—was this contradiction fully overcome. Only there did you fully "shake off" the philosopher and cause the philosopher to give way to the man.

The emphasis by 1844, as will be seen, was not on the human race, but rather on the conscious desires of each sentient individual. Feuerbach no longer saw religion's God as the embodiment of characteristics of the human species, but rather as the means for the satisfaction of individual desires and wishes.

In this sense, *The Essence of Faith According to Luther* foreshadowed the future course of Feuerbach's thought. It was in this essay that he first hit on the conception which would allow him to broaden his study to include nature-worshiping religions. At the end of the essay he indicated that he was about to write a special treatise on this subject; what resulted was *The Essence of Religion* of 1845, embodying the new view. He anticipated also the final stage of his religious investigations when he saw religion as primarily a device for the fulfillment of human wishes. The very terms later used in the *Theogonie*—"urge

toward happiness," "self-love"—appeared importantly
for the first time in this work. There was also a reflec-
tion of Feuerbach's interest in the question of personal
immortality, an interest which showed itself from
1830 to 1866 in a series of writings which indicate,
perhaps more concretely than any other source, the
subtle shifts in Feuerbach's viewpoints through the
years.

The Luther essay offers a typical example of the
style and method used by Feuerbach in his major
works. The emphasis on a nontechnical, colloquial,
personal tone; the irony; the emphasis on loosely or-
ganized, aphoristic construction; the liberal use of
double and multiple adjectives; the love of antitheses
and rhetorical questions; the favorite device of com-
menting upon texts—all these characteristics run
throughout Feuerbach's works. By 1844, Feuerbach
felt the need to provide a more concrete version of the
ideas of *The Essence of Christianity;* that is, one based
on specific statements the reader could see before him,
for he always assumed that by seeing the texts he had
used to substantiate his theories, the reader would immediately consider these theories self-evident. But the
author himself was not sure that he had succeeded in
this attempt. In a valid bit of self-criticism, he ad-
mitted to a friend:

> It is, although sound in its viewpoint, carelessly
> written; and the contradiction in my praiseworthy
> style—obstinate brevity, which doesn't want to say

what it can say, and persevering verbosity, which is never content to say a thing once—comes out even more strikingly in a shorter work. . . . My *Luther* is less colloquial and clear than I had intended when I began to write. And, besides, the conclusion (partly involuntarily, partly consciously) is expressed indirectly.

But not even the most violent opponent of Feuerbach's would accuse him of being reticent or of lacking imagination.

III. THE ESSENCE OF FAITH ACCORDING TO LUTHER—ITS CONTENTS

The subject of the Luther essay, as the full title indicates, is the nature of Christian faith. Feuerbach's assumption was that the ostensible objects of human faith and worship were merely false fronts for other objects dear to the hearts of the believers. What he believed he had done in all his studies was to provide the "key" to the mystery; that is, to discover what really underlay these false fronts. The question he had asked in *The Essence of Christianity* was: "What are Christians really doing when they express a belief in God?" The answer, briefly, was that they were actually expressing a desire for various unattainable ideals, and positing a God embodying these ideals as an assurance of their existence. The attributes of this

God, as mentioned, were actually those of the human race as a whole; thus God's beneficence to man was merely an expression of the love of man for man. In *The Essence of Faith According to Luther* the argument proceeded one step further in the direction, as seen, of emphasizing the human individual. His question now was: "What really motivates the Christian in his belief in God?" and the answer was: "Human egoism, or self-love." His own statement of the main thought of the essay ran as follows:

I have shown you [in *The Essence of Christianity*] that the Supreme Object, which you find and believe in in your God, is the love of man for man. In doing so, I have taken care of you and your God inadequately. But that is not enough for you. You want to believe in something separate from yourselves, something ineffable. But what is this thing you distinguish from love? It is your dear ego, which distinguishes itself from love and is concerned only with itself. Thus love is merely your morality; but your religion, your essence, your God, is self-love. But if you insist on denying this, then find the determining factor and the final goal of your life attained in love, and give up your immortal self. But by "love" I mean activity of body and soul—living for others, for humanity, for universal ends. But since these universal ends only find their actuality and truth in concrete human form (for example, if I want freedom, I want really free men; I do not want freedom merely thought about or intended; I want a visible and tangible freedom), I always frankly posit man as the alpha and omega.

Behind the Christian belief in God, as the chief motivating force of this belief, was human self-love.

Feuerbach demonstrated this by exhibiting statements from various works of Martin Luther which "gave away" the truth behind Luther's doctrine; statements, that is, which would show that the primary purpose of the existence of God is the satisfaction of human desires. His method, then, was to draw a generalization from a number of passages of Luther's, then to present the "documentary evidence," then to proceed to the next stage in the argument. The validity of this method is outside the scope of this introduction; it is left for the reader to decide whether Feuerbach's constructions are convincing. He certainly took Luther's statements out of context, and it may be questioned whether merely explaining why people believe in God really proves anything about God's existence. But the reader is left to think out such controversial points for himself; the latter point, incidentally, is a fundamental criticism which may be leveled against most of his works.

The argument is fairly clear and straightforward, interrupted seldom by disgressions but frequently by clusters of excerpts from Luther's works. He begins by stating that on the surface the Lutheran doctrine places man in a low, degraded position, and hence would appear to contradict the main point of *The Essence of Christianity*—that in religion men exalt humanity above all things. But there is actually no contradiction; rather, Lutheranism confirms Feuerbach's position.

(Pages 31–41) First of all, he points out, Luther asserts a fundamental cleavage or opposition between man and God. Their attributes are mutually exclusive; for otherwise—if we had the same characteristics as God—there would be no need at all for a God. It is no argument to state that we may share some of God's attributes by possessing them in a lesser degree; some attributes, says Feuerbach, exist only in a superlative degree and are hence absolute—that is, either possessed or not. God and man, then, are fundamentally opposed; and Luther, Feuerbach indicates, openly declares himself for God and against man.

(Pages 41–62) But beneath the surface Luther is really on the side of man after all. For Luther does not deny to men the possibility of satisfying their desires. All he does is say that it is God and not man himself who will provide this satisfaction of human wishes. Lutheranism, unlike Catholicism, places all its emphasis on God as a being who is out for the good of man. It is this God—the God looking out for human welfare—who is the object of faith to Luther. All of God's attributes derive from this divine function, including his being the Creator and his omnipotence.

God, then, is essentially a being who satisfies human wishes. Man's wishes are thus primary in the religious order of things. It is the will of man that determines the will of God, as Feuerbach stated elsewhere.

(Pages 62–95) If God is by nature good to man, Feuerbach next states, he must be an essentially human being—and not only in intention, but in actuality. This is the explanation of the Incarnation, or God in human form as Christ. Christ is a living, tangible, sensual proof of God's goodness to man; he shows the certainty of God's benevolence toward men. For this reason, the believer is concerned only with God as Christ—the visible God—and not at all with God-in-himself. Feuerbach rests on this point for some time. Christ, being a human being, can love man and forgive (for he can understand) human sins. God-in-himself cannot. Christ is thus a Mediator between man and God-in-himself, combining characteristics of both as the God-Man. It was this assertion—that the only important aspect of divinity to man is God as a sensual being—which, according to Feuerbach, aroused the bitterest opposition to the essay in 1844.

But the most general and greatest commotion has been caused by the fact that I prove the divine being to be a sensual being, and on the other hand that sensual beings are divine (that is, true) beings—or at least, if I do not prove it, I posit and present this view, for certainly I am guilty of failing to provide many proofs, explanations, and elucidations of my position. But people take "sensuality" to mean only eating, drinking, and making love, just as they understand by "human" only the weaknesses of individuals and the mutable and arbitrary premises and institutions of the times; and thus they place the true human essence, under the name of the divine, opposite man, as a separate kind of being distinguished from man.

(Pages 95–117) The major point of the essay, then, has been made with the assertion that God exists for man's sake. The rest of the essay is an elucidation of the reason men make this assertion; namely, the fact that the basis of the idea of God is human self-love. Faith is synonymous with the belief in God, which is itself the same as the certainty that God is essentially a being that loves man; or, to look at the equation from the other side, the certainty that love for man is the Supreme Good, hence is the very essence of God, is the very basis of faith. But Christians have customarily separated faith and love by stating that the object of faith is God and the object of love is man. Feuerbach shows that this is not true either. Rather, the object of faith is also love—God's love for man—and thus man is the object of faith also. The secret or key of faith is philanthropy—love toward mankind. The only difference between faith and love is that in love *another* man is the object of my attention, whereas in faith I myself am the object of my attention. The object—albeit an indirect one—of faith is thus self-love. Self-love is thus proclaimed the Supreme Good, and God is self-love (or the urge toward happiness) fulfilled. God is the personification of the universal desire for perfect satisfaction of desires, or "blessedness." The attribution of blessedness to God is the certainty that my desire for blessedness is backed up by God—or, what amounts to the same thing, that I myself am divine. Faith, says Feuerbach, changes the "There is a God or Christ" to "I am God or Christ." God makes my innermost wishes valid, just as another human being external to me corroborates or validates my opinions in everyday life. God acts upon me as another human being: he shows me my own nature, fulfills my wishes, corroborates my desires. God is the blessedness of man as fulfilled, or as an actual and objective being. Blessedness—the satisfaction of individual human desires—is the supreme goal of the Christian faith. So the essence of faith as distinguished from love, in the last analysis, is the essence of human self-love. If faith sometimes demands sacrifices of man, these are only sacrifices of temporal well-being in favor of the infinitely superior eternal well-being. Thus, Luther has been forced to admit, one might say, that the reason men believe in God is so that they may be certain of the gratification of their own pleasures. The alpha and omega of religious faith, its starting point and final goal, is man.

IV. "COMMENTS UPON SOME REMARK-
ABLE STATEMENTS BY LUTHER"

It is this idea which is treated from a number of stand-
points in the brief selection which fills out this volume,
"Comments upon Some Remarkable Statements by
Luther" ("Merkwürdige Äusserungen Luthers nebst
Glossen"). Dated the same year as the Luther essay,
the document is clearly a collection of quotations
which did not fit easily into the longer work. But although inessential to the main argument of the longer
work, and despite its grab-bag character, the piece is
not without interest to us. Nowhere did Feuerbach
summarize with more pregnancy and vigor his "discoveries" concerning the human basis of religious
belief, its illogic, and its ultimately dangerous effects.
Nowhere did he revel more gleefully in the substantia-
tions of these discoveries by a great Christian theo-
logian. Nowhere, finally, did he abandon himself
more completely to the rhetorical question and the
exclamation as part of a direct, hard-hitting polemic.

V. THE PRESENT TRANSLATION

This is a translation of the version of *Das Wesen des
Glaubens im Sinne Luthers* that Feuerbach himself
prepared for the first volume of his *Complete Works*,
published by Otto Wigand in Leipzig, in 1846. There
are two other editions—the original edition of 1844
(by the same publisher), and that in the so-called

"second edition" of the *Complete Works* edited by Bolin and Jodl, which is simply a rearranged and reset edition with no critical scholarly apparatus. The translator has carefully compared the 1844 with the 1846 version and found no reason to prefer the former; the dozen changes are all either stylistic improvements or minor modifications of the Luther citations (mostly brief additions). The earlier edition bears the subtitle "A Supplement [*Beitrag*] to *The Essence of Christianity*."

The most obvious liberty which has been taken is the rearrangement of the quotations from Luther. In the original, these were simply part of the text, set off only by quotation marks. Since many of these are long, it seemed advisable to use the device now customary and set them off more strikingly by indentation without using quotation marks.

Although the paragraphs remain unaltered, there has been considerable change in the sentences. The older conventions in regard to punctuation have become obsolete, and it seemed best to follow modern usage. Complex sentences are not so well-loved in the twentieth century, and many of the longer sentences have been broken up into two or even three sentences. Possibly there has been less consistency in transferring from the older devices to the newer ones than might be desirable, but this has not damaged the fidelity to the original, in the translator's judgment.

For a German philosopher living in the shadow of Hegel, Feuerbach offers surprisingly few problems of vocabulary. He makes virtually no use of technical philosophical jargon, and the only problems are the ordinary ones of translating from German. The word *Wesen* means "essence," "being," or "nature," and has had to be translated variously; this has destroyed the force of some plays on words. The noun *Sinnlichkeit* has no exact counterpart in English because the adjective form *sinnlich* has none: not "sensuous," "sentient," or "sensual" fits precisely in all cases. On the strength of Feuerbach's use of the word *Sensualismus* as a synonym (not in this essay, but in other works), the translation "sensualism" or "sensuality" has usually been used. "Blessedness" seemed the best translation of *Seligkeit*, and "faith" for *Glaube*, although the latter sometimes had to be translated "belief."

The capitalization of nouns and pronouns referring to the deity offered a minor problem. The translator, somewhat arbitrarily, capitalized "God" and "Christ" throughout and all pronouns referring to God in the excerpts from Luther but not in the main text. The justification for this, rightly or wrongly, was that, in his opinion, Luther would capitalize references were he writing in English, whereas Feuerbach would not. On the other hand, not to capitalize "God" and "Christ" when it is Feuerbach who is speaking would make it appear that Feuerbach was more of a crusading and militant antitheist than he actually was. Similarly, "incarnation" and "revelation," when used to refer to divine acts, were generally capitalized also, if only because this provided a certain emphasis that helped him clarify Feuerbach's meaning.

VI. FOR FURTHER READING

There is very little by or about Feuerbach in English. There is no standard biography in English or German, and the closest thing to a complete exposition of his works in English is William Chamberlain, *Heaven Wasn't His Destination; the Philosophy of Ludwig Feuerbach* (London, 1941), which is relatively brief. The seventh chapter of Sidney Hook, *From Hegel to Marx* (New York, 1950), is a well-known brief statement, but must be used cautiously. Friedrich Engel's *Ludwig Feuerbach and the Outcome of Classical German Philosophy* is available in several English editions, but is primarily a statement of Marxist philosophy rather than a study of Feuerbach. The present translator's doctoral dissertation, "Ludwig Feuerbach and the Intellectual Basis of Nineteenth Century Radicalism," is an attempt to place Feuerbach's philosophical and religious studies in the context of his radical political and social ideology. The dissertation is available on microfilm. As far as translations are concerned, until very recently there was only the old, and very good, translation of *The Essence of Christianity* by George Eliot, which has been issued in two paperback editions, one containing the entire work and the other greatly condensed but well edited by F. W. Strothmann and E. Graham Waring. It is now possible to read in English Feuerbach's *Philosophy of*

the Future (Library of Liberal Arts, 1966) as well as
the companion volume to the present publication, a
new translation by Ralph Manheim of the lectures
Feuerbach delivered in Heidelberg in 1848–1849,
Lectures on the Essence of Religion (Harper &
Row, 1967).

The opportunities for further reading in other
languages are somewhat better. The closest things to
biographies are both by Wilhelm Bolin, *Ludwig
Feuerbach: sein Wirken und seine Zeitgenossen*
(Stuttgart, 1891), and the long introduction to his
edition of Feuerbach's letters (Leipzig, 1904), recently made available again. The three standard studies
of Feuerbach's works are: Albert Lévy, *La philosophie de Feuerbach et son influence sur la littérature
allemande* (Paris, 1904); Gregor Nüdling, *Ludwig
Feuerbachs Religionsphilosophie, "Die Auflösung der
Theologie in Anthropologie"* (1936); and S. Rawido-
wicz, *Ludwig Feuerbachs Philosophie: Ursprung und
Schicksal* (1931). All three are excellent and exhibit a
fine understanding of the subject; but each is somewhat restricted in scope, as the titles reveal. For
Feuerbach's own writings, there are two editions of
Sämtliche Werke, neither really complete. The first,
as mentioned above, was edited by Feuerbach him-
self, and appeared from 1846 to 1866, published by
Wigand in Leipzig. The present essay appears in
Volume I, *The Essence of Christianity* in Volume
VII. The second edition, edited by Bolin and Jodl
(Stuttgart, 1903–1911), was not a critical edition, and

hence, aside from the valuable introductions and the few pieces not included in the original edition, is not to be preferred to the original edition. It too has been recently reprinted. There are two collections of letters: one, edited by Wilhelm Bolin, *Augsewählte Briefe von und an Ludwig Feuerbach* (2 volumes; Leipzig, 1904), is very complete; the other, Karl Grün, *Ludwig Feuerbach in seinem Briefwechsel und Nachlass, sowie in seiner philosophischen Charakterentwickling* (2 volumes; Leipzig, 1875), contains much additional material, including the Moleschott review of 1850.

THE ESSENCE OF
FAITH ACCORDING
TO LUTHER

Das Wesen des Glaubens im
Sinne Luthers. Ein Beitrag zum
"Wesen des Christenthums." (1844)

The Lutheran religious doctrine contradicts human understanding, sense, and feeling more than any other; indeed, it does this consciously and intentionally. It would seem, therefore, that none provides a greater refutation of the fundamental thoughts of *The Essence of Christianity*,[1] and that none indicates to a greater degree the extrahuman and superhuman origin of its contents; for how could man by himself develop

---

[1] [Editor's note: See the Introduction. Briefly, the fundamental thought of *The Essence of Christianity* was that men "create" a God as the embodiment of certain *human* characteristics they adore.]

a doctrine which degrades and debases man to the extreme, which unqualifiedly denies him, at least before God (i.e., in the highest, and therefore the only decisive, instance), all honor, all merit, all virtue, all power of will, all validity and credibility, all reason and judgment? This would seem to be the case; but the appearance is not the reality.

God and man L. says, are opposed to each other:

If we men describe correctly our position in regard to God, we will discover that between God and us men there is a great difference, and a greater one than between heaven and earth; indeed, there can be no comparison made. God is eternal, just, holy, veracious, and *in summa* God is everything good. Man, on the other hand, is mortal, unjust, deceitful, full of vice, sin, and depravity. Everything in connection with God is good; in connection with man there is death, devil, and hellish fire. God is from eternity and remains in eternity. Man is rooted in sins and lives amid death every moment. God is full of Grace; man is full of disgrace and under the wrath of God. This is the result of comparing man to God (*34* II:497–498).[2]

[2] [Editor's note: At this point Feuerbach, in a note, identified the source of the quotations as the 23-volume Leipzig edition of Luther's WORKS (1729–1740). The quotations have in this translation been converted to the more recent and widely available Weimar edition, Luther, WERKE: *kritische Gesamtausgabe* (Weimar, 1883). In a small number of instances the passages referred to could not be identified with certainty; in these few cases, the references remain in Feuerbach's own notation—they are easily identified by the Roman numerals indicating the volume number. Volume numbers in the Weimar edition are

To every lack in man there is opposed a perfection in God; God is and has exactly what man is not and has not. Whatever is attributed to God is denied to man, and contrariwise whatever one gives to man one takes from God. If man, for example, is the source of his own education and is autonomous (self-legislating), then God is not a legislator, is not a teacher or a revealer; if God does perform these tasks, on the other hand, then man cannot be a teacher and legislator. The less God is, so much more is man; the less man is, so much more is God.

If you want to have God, therefore, give up man; if you want to have man, reject God—or else you have neither of the two. The nullity of man is the presupposition of the reality of God. To affirm God is to negate man; to honor God is to scorn man; to praise God is to revile man. The glory of God rests only on the lowliness of man, divine blessedness only on human misery, divine wisdom only on human folly, divine power only on human weakness.

It is God's nature that He manifests His divine majesty and power through nullity and weakness. He Himself says to Paul, 2 Cor. 12, "My strength is made perfect in weakness" (45:222).

My power can be powerful only in your weakness. If thou wilt not be weak, My power has nothing to

given in italic arabic numbers. A few references are from the Weimar *Briefwechsel* and are identified by *Br.* before the volume number.]

do with thee. If I am to be thy Christ and thou Mine Apostle, thou shalt have to reconcile thy weakness with My strength, thy folly with My wisdom, My life with thy death (44:587).

To God alone belong justice, truth, wisdom, strength, holiness, blessedness, and everything good. But our lot is injustice, folly, lying, weakness, and everything evil, all of which is proven superfluously in Scripture. For "all men are liars" it says in Psalms 116, 11; and in Hosea 13, "O Israel, thou hast destroyed thyself." Thus we all are deficient in the glory which we ought to have before God, so that no human being may glory before Him, as Paul says in Romans 3, etc. For this reason the honor of God cannot be told without at the same time telling of the shame of men. And God cannot be praised as veracious and just and merciful if we are not openly declared to be liars and sinners and miserable people.

Either-Or.

Either a devil to men—"all men except Christ are children of the Devil" (37:411), but an angel to God—"Christ and Adam (i.e., God and man) are to be considered in their relation to each other as angel and devil" (46:639); or a devil to God, but an angel to men. If man is free, true, and good, then it is to no purpose that God is good, true, and free; there is no necessity, no reason, for God to be so. The necessity of a God in general rests only on the fact that he is and has what we are not and have not. If we are what he is, what is the need of him? Whether he is or is not is immaterial. We gain nothing through his being, and lose nothing through his not being; for we have in God only a repetition of ourselves. God's existence is an intellectual necessity, an emotional need, only when those qualities which are in God and make him God would not exist if God himself did not exist. But this is only the case when the essential qualities (i.e., those which make God God), such as wisdom, goodness, justice, truth, freedom, are not also in us; for if they are also in us, they remain in us whether God is or not, and there is nothing essentially interesting connected with the acceptance of a God. Only when a sharp, acute distinction—or rather opposition—subsists between us and God do we avoid being indifferent to the question whether he exists or not.

"We do not abolish the distinction between God and us," I hear men of limited intellect interject, "when we ascribe to men goodness, freedom, and other divine qualities, for we attribute these qualities to men only in a limited or lower degree, but to God in the highest degree." But a faculty, power, or quality which is actually capable by its nature of augmentation—not all qualities are naturally or rationally capable of augmentation—deserves to be recognized as what it is and called by its characteristic name only when it reaches its highest degree. The superlative in this case is actually the true positive. Only the highest degree of freedom is freedom—undoubted, decided, true freedom, in accord with the concept of freedom.

Whatever is capable of augmentation still wavers between itself and its opposite, between being and nonbeing. Thus, for example, an artist of lesser (and consequently augmentable) rank wavers between being an artist and being a nonartist. Only an artist of the first rank is unqualifiedly and uncontestably an artist; only the final, uttermost degree, only the extreme, is always the truth. If, therefore, God is the supremely good thing, the freest thing, then you must recognize that he alone is good and free, and you must send your limited freedom and your limited goodness to the devil.

> Free will is not attributable to man, but is rather a divine possession, which no one must or may bear but the Supreme Divine Majesty alone, for God the Lord alone does, as Psalm 115 says, whatever He pleases, in heaven, on earth, on the sea, and in all the depths. If I say this about a man, it is the same as if I said, "A man has divine force and strength"; that would be the greatest blasphemy on earth and a theft of the Divine Honor and Name.

> Because of this, if one values Grace and the aid of Grace, it is also preached that the free will can do nothing. And it is a good, strong, firm, certain consequence if I say, "Scripture values God's Grace alone; therefore the free will is nothing" (*18*:755).

> But what is valid concerning free will or the grace

of God—for grace is nothing but divine will—is also valid concerning all other attributes of God and in regard to God himself. Divinity, the praiseworthiness and venerability of God, rests only on the fact that he has what we do not have, for what one has oneself, one does not treasure and value. If man were blessed— blessed in the rapturous sense, as the Christian desires to be—how could he imagine another being outside himself as a blessed being and because of this attribute make it an object of his honor and prayer? Only an imprisoned man considers a free man blessed; only a sick man considers a healthy man blessed. Blessedness exists only in the imagination, not in actuality; only in the idea of possession, not in possession itself. Only as the object of an idea, only at a distance, only in separation does the trivial become ideal, the earthly celestial, the human divine. Past happiness is holy to us, not present happiness; the dead man, not the living man. In short, an object is holy only as long as it is an object in thought and not in actuality. For this reason, all natural bodies were objects of religious reverence as long as they were only objects of thought, of the imagination, and not of actual scientific observation, through which they become known to man as they actually are. Thus the stars were objects of religious reverence to the Greeks; that is, they did not see the stars as stars, but imagined them to be supermundane living beings. But some Greek philosophers hurled these gods from their thrones. That is, they transferred the stars from the heaven of imagination to the earth of scientific observation; they recognized their actual similarity to the profane earth. Whoever, therefore, attributes to man qualities of God, i.e., changes divine attributes from objects of thought to objects of actuality, of possession—whoever does this abolishes not only the celestial magic of religion, but also the need of a God, the very foundation of religion. Religion, of course, is the bond between God and man; but like every bond, it rests only on a need, on a lack. But if I have what God has, nothing is lacking if God is lacking. However, it is only if something is lacking to me when God is lacking that God is a necessity for me. Blessedness is a need only for a wretched man, freedom only for a slave, and only man's servitude is in accord with God's freedom. If, on the other hand, I am free, I am above all else free from God. The homage granted to God by a free person is at best only a protestation of courtesy, a gallantry, a compliment. Only in the needy, miserable, and deprived mouth does the word "God" have weight, earnestness, and meaning; but on the lips of the religiously free men—on the politically free men's too, of course—the word "God" rings only of scorn.

It is thus impossible for man to be what God is, if God is not to be a mere luxury article. This impossibility, this necessity that every affirmation in God presupposes a negation in man, is the foundation on which Luther erected his edifice and shattered the Roman Catholic church. If God is good, then man is evil, and it is consequently blasphemy, a denial of God, if man ascribes good actions and good works to himself. For good comes only from the good, "good fruit presupposes a good tree"; therefore whoever gives himself credit for good works confers upon himself a good nature, claims a divine attribute, and in actuality makes himself a God. If God is himself the mediator of man with God, if God is the Savior, the Redeemer, the Sanctifier, then man cannot be the redeemer of his own sins, his own savior. And consequently all the so-called meritorious works performed by man—all the sufferings and martyrdoms which he places upon himself in order to absolve his sins, to reconcile himself with God, and to attain divine grace and bliss—are vain and invalid. Vain and invalid, therefore, are the rosary, the lenten fare, the pilgrimage, the mass, the sale of indulgences, the monk's hood, the nun's veil.

If we can redeem a sin with works and thus obtain Grace, then Christ's blood has flowed without need and cause (*12*:155)[3]

According to the Jewish faith, it is through works and self-action that the Grace of God is obtained, sin is expiated and blessedness attained. In this scheme Christ must be excluded, since He is not

[3] By works L. understands not only external, ceremonial, and religious works, but also moral works. See L.'s *Letters, Epistles, and Reflections*, edited by de Wette, *Br. 1*:69; and L.'s *Works, 50*:598, and XVII, 44–45. [Editor's note: All notes are Feuerbach's unless otherwise indicated.]

necessary or at least not very necessary. They say they want to expiate their sin and become blessed through a stern life; they give to works and to the spiritual leaders what belongs to Christ and to faith alone. What else is this but to deny Christ (*10* II: 148)?

Where do the Papists lead this faith? Actually to themselves. For they teach men to trust to their merits. None of the Papists and monks calls himself Christ; none of them says "I am called and wish to be called and named Christ." But they say all the same "I am Christ." They withhold the name from themselves, but they attribute to themselves the position, the power, and the person (*8*: 599).

What shall God forgive if we ourselves do enough to atone for all our sins (*6*: 626)?

If it were for the sake of our repentance that sins were forgiven, the honor would be ours and not God's (*7*: 376–377).

These two do not suffer themselves to be together nor can they be together—namely, believing that we have God's Grace for Christ's sake without our meriting it, and considering that we must also attain it through works. For if it could be merited through us, we would not need Christ for it (XIII, 657).

Of the two one must collapse: if I rest on God's Grace and mercy, I do not rest on my merit and works; and contrariwise, if I rest on my works and merits, I do not rest on God's Grace (*12*:*556*).

Grace or Merit. Grace abolishes merit; merit abolishes grace. But grace is a result of faith, merit of works; and faith is from God, works from man. For in faith I give evidence of God; in works I give evidence of myself, a functioning man. So you must be concerned either with God or with man; either believe in God and doubt man, or believe in man and doubt God. You cannot at the same time believe in and doubt God, at the same time beg for benevolent support and possess ability yourself, at the same time be both servant and master, at the same time both Lutheran and Papist. Either entirely for God and against man, or else entirely for man and against God.

Now Luther declares himself entirely, unqualifiedly—L. is every inch a man—for God and against man. God, as we have seen, is everything to him, man nothing.[4] God is virtue, beauty, sweetness, power, health, amiability; man is personified depravity, contrariness, hatefulness, worthlessness, and uselessness. Luther's doctrine is divine but inhuman, indeed barbaric—a hymn to God, but a lampoon of man.

But it is only inhuman at its starting point, not as it develops; in its presuppositions, not in its consequences; in its means, not in its end.

Only the thirsty person feels the benefit of drink;

---

[4] The expression that man or a creature is nothing compared with God, because they were created by him *ex nihilo,* is often found in Luther, e.g., *43*:178–179.

only the hungry person feels the benefit of food. There is no satisfaction and no enjoyment without a need. Of course, hunger is in itself pain and torment—hunger deprived of food. But hunger cannot exist without its object, food. It is self-defeating; it has its purpose not in itself but in its opposite, in its own satisfaction. Is a being miserable and invalid, therefore, because it is subject to hunger pangs? Not at all; for this suffering is a suffering aimed at his benefit, a woe which leads to well-being, a need striving for enjoyment. A being would only be truly miserable and invalid if it were condemned permanently to hunger, and consequently to nonbeing, for unsatisfied hunger ends only with the end of man. But this assumption—except in unusual cases, which are not to be counted—is absurd; it destroys its own force. For the meaning of hunger is the enjoyment of food; hunger is nothing more than the desire for food.

The very same thing is true of the Lutheran doctrine. It places you in the condition of hunger, where all man's powers are denied him, his courage sinks, his self-esteem disappears, where he cries out full of doubt, "Alas, a man without food is truly nothing at all!" But it places you in this inhuman condition only to encourage—by hunger—the enjoyment of food:

The Lord Christ likes no one but a hungry and thirsty soul. Food is not needed by a satiated soul (*16:221*).

Those like it best, however, who lie in the struggle

with death, or whom an evil conscience presses—
there hunger is a good cook, as they say, who
makes food taste good. But those stubborn people
who live in their own holiness, who count on their
works, and who do not perceive their sins and misfortune: these people do not like it. Whoever sits
at a table and is hungry likes everything; someone
who is already full likes nothing, but rather dislikes
even the best food (*12*:304–305).

No food without hunger, so also no grace without
sin,[5] no salvation without need, no God who is everything without man who is nothing. What hunger
takes away, food provides again. What Luther takes
away from you in your human condition, he replaces
for you a hundredfold in God.

Luther is inhuman toward man only because he has
a humane God and because the humanity of God
takes away man's own humanity from him. If man
has what God has, God is superfluous; man fills the
place of God. But the reverse is also true: if God has
what man has, God fills the place of man, and thus it
is not necessary for man to be man. If God thinks for
man—and he does this whenever he reveals himself or
expresses himself (i.e., tells man in advance what man
is to repeat to him, what he is to think of him)—then
man does not have to think for himself. If God is a

[5] "As long as they will not admit to sin and being evil where they
actually are, they will also not admit as grace what is actually grace,
through which sin can be removed. A man who will not admit being
ill will not consider medicine as medicine" (7:449).

being who acts for man and for his welfare and
blessedness, then man's activity for himself is superfluous—God's action makes mine unnecessary.

> If Christ does it, I may not do it. One of the two
> must be stopped—either Christ or my own action
> (37:46).

If God cares for you and loves you, your care for
yourself and your self-esteem are unnecessary. If God
carries you in his hands, you do not have to stand and
move on your own legs. And you will attain your
goal just as well—indeed, better—in someone else's
hands as on your own legs.

> Go away, you loathsome Devil! You want to en-
> courage me to care for myself, although God says
> everywhere, "I will care for him Myself," and says,
> "I am your God"; that is to say, "I will care for
> you; consider Me thus and let Me take care of
> you." As Saint Peter says, "Throw all your cares
> on Him, for He cares for you." And David:
> "Throw your anxieties upon the Lord, Who will
> care for you." The loathsome Devil, who is the
> enemy of God and Christ, wants to force us upon
> ourselves and our own care, so that we might under-
> take God's office (which is to care for us and to be
> our God) (*Br.* 6:87–88).

Wherever Christ's disciples are, they do not have
to do anything for themselves and for their sin and
for their blessedness, but rather Christ's blood has

already done this and accomplished it; and He loved them, so that they no longer have to love themselves, nor seek nor wish for anything good (*12*:149).

Your eyes should be closed concerning yourself, while My eyes are open concerning you (*1*:172).

God and man stand in the same relation to each other as husband and wife—a comparison often used by Luther and by Christians generally. If my wife cooks, washes, spins for me, I myself do not have to cook, spin, or wash. Where my wife is active, I am inactive; where she is something, I am nothing. In general, what I have in my wife, I need not have in myself; for whatever is the wife's is also the husband's, even though the wife is another being, separate from the husband. If the husband, therefore, wants to be and do himself what his wife is and does for him, if he wants to substitute himself for his wife, he insults himself disgracefully. Now if I prevent man from self-satisfaction, am I therefore inhumanly barbaric toward him? Certainly not; for I am not keeping him from satisfaction. I am only keeping him from satisfying himself, from seeking in himself what he should seek outside himself and naturally can find only outside himself.

Exactly the same thing is true of God. What you have in God, you do not have in and by yourself, but you still have it. It is yours—of course, not as your arm or your leg are yours, but as your wife is yours.

It belongs to you not as an attribute, but as an object; however, as an object which is not yours accidentally, but rather essentially, for it has precisely what you lack, and therefore belongs to you yourself. God is what you are not; but just because of this he is as indispensable to you as food is to hunger, drink to thirst, a wife to a husband. And it is precisely *because* you have that very lack that he is what you are not. God is veracious because we are liars, good because we are evil, humane and human because we are wild beasts. Man completes and satisfies himself in God; man's defective nature is a perfect nature in God. Seek and ye shall find. What you miss in Luther's conception of man you will find in God. What we have lost completely as an object of self-activity and will—the human essence—radiates forth before us as an object of faith in the form of the divine essence. Man in himself is and can do nothing, but in God (that is, through faith) he is and can do everything—he even has power over God. "God does the will of the believer."[6]

Considered superficially, the Lutheran faith is no different from the Catholic faith in its essential object and content. God, as in the Nicene Creed, "became man for us men and for the sake of our blessedness; for us He was crucified, suffered, was buried, and resurrected"—this is the basic article of the Lutheran as well as of the Catholic faith. Luther has only

[6] Quotations without references have been used in *The Essence of Christianity;* citations as to sources will be found there.

brought to light again the doctrinal system of Augustine, the most influential of the Catholic Church Fathers. How could there, then, be an important distinction in essential content between Luther and the Catholic Church? But Luther departs from the old story immediately in placing all his emphasis upon the "for the sake of us men," upon the "for us"; in making not the Incarnation, the Resurrection, the Passion of Christ in themselves the essential content and object of faith, but rather the Incarnation *for us*, the Passion of Christ *for us*, while the Catholics were more concerned with the mere fact, with the object itself.

Thus the Catholics took to heart only the fact that Christ suffered, but not that he suffered for us. Of course, they too recognized it as a moving, indeed a rapturous, idea that God had suffered for men's sake, but this was not a practical truth, pregnant with results. Were it so they would not have concluded from the suffering of Christ the necessity of their own suffering in order to attain blessedness and reconciliation with God. For if Christ has actually suffered for us, our own suffering is superfluous and in vain; what was to be attained through our suffering has already been attained through Christ's suffering, or else—a frightening "or else"—Christ has suffered to no end. But no, his suffering is sufficient; it removes the need for our suffering. His suffering is our suffering. If he has suffered for us, we have already suffered in him; if I act for others, I act in their place and relieve them of the necessity of doing for themselves what I have done for them. But if I consider the Passion of Christ only an example, which I am to imitate and repeat through my own suffering, I make suffering itself an object, I give it independent significance. However, suffering in itself was not the object and purpose of Christ's Passion; the object, rather, was *our* salvation, *our* redemption. He has suffered *for us;* that is to say, he has freed us and redeemed us from suffering. Of course, Luther too would have us keep before us the Passion of Christ as an example, so that we may suffer patiently and submissively, as he did, at least while we linger in this vale of tears where the consequences of Christ's Redemption are by no means completely objectified. But this suffering of ours is not a suffering for the purpose of reconciliation and redemption; it has only moral power and significance, and no longer religious power and significance, as was true in Catholicism. Not outside us, then, not in the object of faith itself, but *in us* lie the purpose and meaning of this object of faith. Not that Christ is Christ, but that he is Christ *for you;* not that he died or that he suffered, but that he died *for you*, suffered *for you*—that is the main point.

> What have we produced in the Papacy? We have acknowledged that He (Christ) is God and man; but that He is *our* Savior, Who has died and arisen and so forth *for us*, we have denied with all our might (50:268).

A woman who lives without marriage can indeed say, "There is a husband"; but she cannot say that it is her husband. Thus we can all indeed say that this is a God, but we do not all say that He is *our* God (*14*:16).

It is therefore not enough that a man believe that there is a God, that Christ suffered, etc., but he must firmly believe that God is a God for *his* blessedness, that Christ suffered for *him*, etc. (*11*:472).

Christ is God and Man and He is God and Man so that He may be Christ not for Himself but for us (*10* III:364).

Everything we relate in faith occurred for us and comes home to us (*45*:19).

Although these words which faith must accept—to be born, to suffer, etc., for us—are not expressed (in the Apostolic Creed), we must discover it from other sources and learn from all these pieces, for in the third article where we say, "I believe in the forgiveness of sins," He Himself comments that He sees in this piece the cause and utility of His being born, suffering, and doing everything. And we are also moved by the place in the text where we say, "Our Lord," for we recognize that everything the Man is and does happens for us, when He was

born, suffered, died, and was resurrected as a pledge
that He is our Lord (XVIII, 125).

Here we have expressed in Luther's own words the
difference between the Lutheran faith and the older
faith. What Luther says is, of course, already con-
tained in the older faith, but not outspokenly or expressly, at least not so decidedly, so palpably, so
popularly. Luther was the first to let out the secret of
Christian faith. The word which in the older faith is
only a commentary, Luther makes into the text; the
light which the former hides under the bushel he
places upon the bushel so that it may illuminate the
eyes of everyone. The key to the mysteries of faith
lies in *us*; the riddle of the Christian faith is resolved
in *us*. Not only did God become man for us, not only
did he suffer for us, as is stated in the Nicene Creed,
but he is God for us, omnipotent Creator for us,
Holy Spirit for us. In short, it is for *us* that he is what
he is—the "us" runs through all the articles; the "us"
encompasses and includes all the articles in itself. The
older faith also says, "Our Lord, our God," but it
underlines the "God"; Luther, on the other hand,
underlines the "our." That is, he makes the fact that
he is *ours* an essential attribute of God himself. God
is not God if he is not *our* God. *We* are the salt not
only of the earth but also of heaven. "If God sat in
heaven for Himself alone," says Luther, "like a block,
He would not be God." God is a word the sole meaning of which is "man."

The essence of faith according to Luther consists, then, of the belief that God is by his very nature concerned with man, the belief that God is a being existing not for himself or against us, but rather *for us*, a good being, good *to us men.*

To have God is to have all Grace, all mercy, and everything which one can call good (*14*:16).

The divine nature is nothing but mere beneficence and, as Saint Paul says, friendship and affability—philanthropy (*10* I 1:100–101, 98).

What does it mean to have a God; or, what is God? Answer. A God is that from Whom one should expect all good, and in Whom one should take refuge in times of need. Therefore, to have a God is simply to believe in and trust in Him from the heart; as I have often said, trust and faith of the heart create both God and false god. Whatever you hang your heart upon and trust, that is actually your God. God is the One from Whom one receives all good and relief from all misfortune. Therefore I am pleased that we Germans should call God by the ancient name (finer and more appropriate than any other), "Good," as the One Who is an eternal source overflowing with superabundant good and from Whom everything which is good, and is called good, flows (*30* I:132–133; 135–136).

The works and divine services of all peoples testify

to the fact that to be a God is nothing but to do good to man. For one calls to Jove, and another to Mars, only because they want to be helped by them. However wrong they are in regard to the person of God because of their idolatry, the service is nevertheless there which appertains to the true God; that is, the appeal and that they expect all good and help from Him (*44*:84).

It is God, therefore, who can save me from all moral as well as physical evil, whom I can unqualifiedly rely upon in all times of need. But in order to be an object of unqualified faith and trust, and hence in order to be God or, rather, to be able to be God, a being must be without needs; for a being with needs has enough to do for itself. It must be veracious and unchangeable (in being good); otherwise it is not dependable. It must be omnipresent; otherwise it can help me where it is but not in distant places. It must be knowing—indeed, omniscient—for if it has no eyes and ears, like the pagan statues of gods, it cannot perceive my sorrows. It must be omnipotent and unlimited, for a limitation on its power or its nature in general is also a limitation on my trust. It must be autonomous and independent of all things—indeed, with power over all things—for if it is not Lord of all things, it is not Lord over all evils. All the divine attributes are thus only means to the end of benevolence. God is only omnipotent in order to be omnipotently good, unlimited in order to be unlimitedly good, without needs in order to be selflessly good. All these attributes in themselves, separately or all together, do not make God God. A diabolical being can also be omnipotent and omniscient. It is solely a matter of the heart; God must have a heart. Being good is essential to being God, but being good in the highest and most unlimited sense, being good without the limits which prevent the human individual from being good. For what is a good will without the means and powers to fulfill it; what good does it do? A will without the power to perform is only an impotent wish. What is goodness without omniscience? Only too often goodness does the opposite of what it wants to do, and consequently is a destructive goodness. To be capable of absolute goodness, therefore, one must be a God; that is, a being unlimited and perfect in every respect. Only one who has all power can fulfill all wishes; only one who is in possession of all goods can cure all evils; only one who has everything can give everything.

But God is not good for his own sake. For something to be good, there must be something else to which it is good. A being considered exclusively in terms of itself is neither good nor evil. Evil is that which is against something else; good is that which is for something else. Only he is a good man who is good to another, who does good; in doing good for others he is good in himself. What benefits others is from the well-doer's standpoint a morally good act, just as what harms others is from the evildoer's standpoint an evil act. My reason and power apply to me,

but my goodness applies only to others. Goodness is
not a permanent attribute, but a fluctuating and tran-
sitional one. To be good means to love—love is only
goodness; but is love thinkable without something else
which is loved? Of course, the meaning of an act of
love is solely in the object of that love. But God is
good to us; only in us, therefore, lies the meaning of
God's goodness. It is only for our benefit that God is
good. But all divine attributes are divine only as attributes of a good (and not an evil or diabolical) being. Hence, through goodness, all divine powers and
attributes are for our benefit and welfare; they all
abound for us.

God is an omnipotent creator, the creator of heaven
and earth. This attribute is the first and most pleasing
of the divine attributes, the one which distinguishes
him most particularly from all other beings and which
pertains to him alone. Thus, whatever is true of this
attribute is also true of the others, and all the more
true the less they separate God from man [i.e., the
more God's qualities and man's approach one an-
other]. Now God is not only creator of heaven and
earth, he is also our creator; and it is his being our
creator that provides a meaning and a basis for his
being the creator of heaven and earth. For only in
man is the creation completed, and, according to the
Christian faith, heaven and earth with all they contain
were created for men, not for themselves. God is thus
not a creator for himself nor a creator of nature for
the sake of nature, but a creator for men. He creates

so that we may be; we are the purpose and object of his creative activity. God has us in mind—he wants *us*—when he wants the world. The first divine attribute is also the first proof of God's goodness toward us. So God is not only our creator, but also our Father, and he is only a creator because he cannot be our Father without being a creator. A good will presupposes power; love presupposes physical ability. How can I be good—that is, something—to a being if I am nothing? How can I be a father if I can bring forth no children? How can I be the source of all good if I am not the source of the first good—life or existence?

In any case, the power to create is the expression of a power which "can make everything of nothing and everything once more nothing" (XXI, 419).

> Is it not true that when He speaks the earth becomes such as He commands? And contrariwise, when He speaks, the world becomes nothing and suddenly collapses (*40* II: 236).

This power considered in itself can, in any case, destroy what it has created, just as the human father can destroy his own child. But just as this destructive omnipotence in the form of the human father finds its bounds and limit in humanity, so in the form of God it finds his bounds and limit in divinity, that is, in goodness. God is only evil against evil, in order to be able to be good to goodness. How can God create health if he cannot do away with illness? How can he

revivify if he cannot kill death? How, in general, can
he be for man if he cannot be against that which is
against man? But what is not against man, at least in
certain cases? Everything outside man is potentially
against him, even he himself, as a matter of fact; how
often is a man (consciously and intentionally or un-
consciously and unintentionally) not only against
other men but also against himself? As often as he
sins; and how easily man sins, with very grave consequences—loss of health, of cheerfulness, of peace of
mind, and (even more importantly in the eyes of the
religious person) of the Grace of God, of eternal life!
In order to secure yourself on all sides, therefore, in
order to make yourself inaccessible to all enemies
which may threaten you from within or from without, you must place yourself under the dominion of
an omnipotence, but an omnipotence which is itself
ruled by goodness. You only have the effects in your
power if you have the cause in your power. The only
one who can prevent you from burning amidst a fire
is the one who himself causes the fire to burn. God, by
means of his omnipotent will, has united to fire the
attribute of burning; he can take it away again if he
wishes to do so. God is the Lord of all things, but this
Lord is *your* Lord. All things are from God; this
means that all things are in God's power and (because
God is yours) in your power. Nothing is, or can do,
anything against God—this means that nothing is, or
can do, anything against you, for God exists for you.

 The following quotations from Luther will demonstrate the correctness of this explanation of creation and omnipotence.

God can do everything, but only wishes to do good (XVIII, 304).

God is omnipotent; therefore He wishes us to ask for everything which is useful to us (*20*:720).

Since He (God) is omnipotent, what can I lack which He cannot give me or do for me? Since He is Creator of heaven and earth and Lord of all things, who will take anything from me or harm anything of mine? Indeed, how will all things not be for my benefit and serve me if the one to whom they are all obedient and subjected grants [*gan*; Feuerbach queries *gönnt*?][8] goodness to me (7: 216)?

Whoever has a merciful prince fears nothing which is beneath this prince; he defies it, and praises and recognizes his lord's mercy and power. How much more does a Christian sing praises and defy agony, death, hell, and devil, and say confidently to them, "What can you do to me? Are you not beneath the feet of my Lord?" All things are beneath His feet; who will therefore be against me (*10* I:1; 717)?

Snow, hoar-frost, and coldness are His (He says). He creates them Himself and they are not in the Devil's or the enemy's hands; He is in control of

[8] In the Walch edition (X, 200), it is *gann*.

them. Therefore, they must not be colder, nor chill
us more, than He wants them to be and we can
stand. If the Devil had frost in his hands, not only
would mere winter and personal frost remain forever, and there would be no more summer, but it
would freeze so hard that all men would be frozen
on one day and become mere lumps of ice (*31*
I:448).

I believe in God the Father, Creator of heaven and
earth. This little word "Father" shows us that He
wishes to be both Father and omnipotent Creator.
The animals cannot call him Father, but we are to
call him Father and be known as His children. We
pray for this and recognize it when we say here, in
the article of faith, "I believe in God the Father,
that just as He lives as a Father and eternally, we
also live eternally as His children and are not to
die." Thus we are a much higher and more beauti-
ful creation than the other creatures (*45*:76).

Since God can construct and bring forth heaven
and earth out of water, and since He can create sun
and moon out of a drop of water, is He not capable
of protecting my body against enemies and the
Devil, or, even if it is laid in earth, reawaken it to
a new life? Therefore, we are to learn to recognize
God's omnipotent force and strength from this,
and, indeed, not doubt that all is true which God
has said and commanded in His words. For here we
have a complete confirmation of all divine promises;

namely, that nothing is either so difficult or impossible that God is not able to make it right with His words (42:37).

Omnipotence confirms the divine promises; that is, it says the same thing that is said by the promise of the forgiveness of sins, the promise of the answering of prayers, the promise of the eternal life. But what is the meaning of the promise, for example, that "You will not die"? The fact that I do not wish to die.[9] What would be the purpose of promising me something I do not want and desire? To promise means to say "Yes"; it thus presupposes a request or a wish or a desire in me. So that if omnipotence is the confirmation of divine promises, it must also have as a presupposition or foundation a wish or desire in us. And this is in fact the case. But omnipotence is not based upon a specific wish, as, for example, the promise of eternal life is related to my specific wish that there be no death and no limitation to my existence. It is based rather on the unspecific over-all wish that there be in general no natural necessity, no limitations, no opposition to the human being and to human wishes; it is based on the wish that everything be only for men and nothing against men. The specific divine promises thus are dependent for their confirmation upon omnipotence; for in order that this or that limitation of the human being not be, it is necessary that there be no

[9] [Editor's note: The emphasis on the human wish throughout this paragraph clearly foreshadows Feuerbach's later stress on gods as the means for the fulfillment of human wishes. See the Introduction.]

limitations in general. This or that promise takes this
or that limitation away—as the promise of eternal life
takes away the limitation of time—but omnipotence
takes away all limitations. Every desire or wish has
something opposing it; I wish that something which
exists may not exist or that something else which does
not exist may exist. Thus if I wish to eat, I am opposed by hunger; I wish for hunger, which exists, not
to exist, and I wish for satisfaction, on the other
hand, which does not exist, to exist. Every wish wants
to make nonbeing out of being and being out of nonbeing. Every wish is the wish for omnipotence and
for creation *ex nihilo*, because what I wish for I wish
to be able to do immediately, unqualifiedly, without
materials. But every specific wish is still limited and
bound up with a specific object—thus the essence of
the wish in general is expressed freely and unqualifiedly only in the essence of omnipotence. Omnipotence can do whatever I wish, whatever I imagine;
consequently, it is evident that it can fulfill this and
that specific wish. Unlimited ability presupposes an
unlimited wish; ability without desire is meaningless.
But God has the ability, man the desire. Omnipotence
surpasses the limits of nature and reason; it can do
things which, according to reason, are meaningless,
according to nature, impossible. But it surpasses these
limits solely because human desire surpasses the limits
of nature and reason—of course, in imagination and
ideas and not in truth and actuality.

Let us mention too that the meaning of omnip-

otence and creation developed above is clearly evident also in the belief that nature as it is did not
originally come from God. For in the world as it is
there are all kinds of evil—physical and moral, illness
and sin, death and Devil. But in the world as it was
before it was defaced and ruined by a being opposed
to God (sin, the Devil), as it was when still a pure
work, a pure copy of the divine essence,

> in Paradise, there were no burning nettles, nor
> prickly thorns and thistles, nor dangerous plants,
> worms, nor animals, but only beautiful and noble
> roses and sweet-smelling plants; all trees in the
> Garden were pleasant to look at and good to eat.
> After Adam's fall the world was cursed. It is be-
> cause of this that there have come so many danger-
> ous creatures, which fight against us and torture
> and plague us, even we men amongst ourselves (45:
> 233).

Whatever is against us men can thus not be from God.
Why? Because God is a being only for us, and what
is against us is therefore against God. In any case, this
world subsists with God's will. And this will is good
to man. All evil and suffering which befall man come
not from hatred and animosity but from God's love
to man. Their purpose is only man's well-being—his
eternal well-being, if not his temporal well-being—
and they are therefore not to be accepted by man as
evil, with displeasure and ill humor, but (through
faith in this beneficent purpose and basis) must be

borne with a joyful heart. But, despite these illusions
of faith, this world contradicts human—particularly
Christian—wishes,[10] and it is therefore dissolved by
omnipotence, in order to make way again for that
original (or rather even more splendid, truly divine)
world in which nothing is against man.

"God is a being which exists for us men, which is
good for us men." What does this mean but: "God is
a human-minded being"? How can I be good to a
being if I am not good to him according to his own
wishes? If I wish to be good to a flower, I must do its
will—I must give it the light, warmth, water, and
earth it desires. If I treat it not according to its own
point of view, but according to my own arbitrary
point of view, I am not good to it, but evil. If I wish
to be good to flowers, then, I must be a florist; if I
wish to be good to man, I must be a being good in a
human sense, a human-minded being. "Evil" and "inhuman" are synonymous, as are "good" and "human."
Thus man is the highest good of man, for no being is
so good to man as man. For man there is no other
measure of goodness than man.[11] And this measure—
provided it is not taken of the individual, but of the

---

[10] "Whoever believes, however, that there is a God must soon con-
clude that this life on earth is not everything, but that another eternal
life lies before us. For we see in our experience that God does not
accept this temporal life as pleasant. But God promises us an eternal
life after this one. And it means nothing that He lets us wade around
in this temporal life as if we had no God Who would or could help
us. For His assistance is to be an eternal assistance" (52:84).

[11] So that if the supreme principle of Christian morality is "Do
good for God's sake," and the supreme principle of philosophical
morality is "Do good for the sake of the good," the supreme principle
of morality based on man is "Do good for man's sake."

species, which, however, is no object of Christianity *per se*—is in no way an egoistical or a limited one, not even in a physical sense; for man exists as well under the equator as under the polar circles. What would be the death of the human race would also be the death of the plant and animal world, at least that of the present time. An absolutely inhuman heat or cold could not be borne by the animals and plants either. The measure of the species is an absolute one, not a relative one, as is that of individuals and breeds; for what is good and beneficial to one breed is not good and beneficial to another, but the species takes up all these relative measures in itself. What is good for the entire human species is therefore also good for the animal and plant world; it is good in itself.

But what gives us the certainty—the indubitable, irrefragable certainty—that God is actually a being for us, a good, a human-minded being? The appearance of God as a man in Christ, which was by no means a transitory appearance, for even today God is still a man in Christ. In Christ God has revealed himself; that is, he has shown and proved himself to be a human being. In the humanity of Christ the humanness of God is placed beyond all doubt. The chief sign that God is good is that he is a man. "To be good" means "to be a man." I am only good when I sympathize with and take unto myself the suffering of others; but "to sympathize with others and to feel for others" means "to be a man." But there is no feeling, much less sympathy, compassion, commiseration, or mercy, without sensuality. Where there is no ear, there is no complaint; where there is no eye, there is no tear; where there is no lung, there is no sigh; where there is no blood, there is no heart. How can I have access to a person who has no senses? Who can be my representative and mediator without an eye and an ear? The pledge and truth of the goodness and mercy (humanness) of God lie therefore in Christ as the sensual essence of God.

God without flesh is worth nothing (*25*:107).

Indeed, he is, as Luther says in this same place and in many other places, a "frightful image of wrath and death"; for God without flesh is also God against flesh, against man. For what is not valid in God is not valid before God; what God cannot suffer in himself he cannot in general suffer in other beings. What is denied of God, excluded from God, is thereby declared to be something godless, opposed to God, null. If, therefore, there is no flesh in God, flesh is nothing before God. Only man is for man, only flesh for flesh. What is not of my nature is also not of my mind; thus a being not of flesh has no appreciation or feeling for flesh.

All men, Luther often says, think of God as a good and beneficent being, for how would they otherwise call upon God for help in their time of need? Nevertheless, since this good being is for them only a thought of theirs, they fall into doubt as to whether God is *actually* good, and through this doubt into idolatry. But Christians have more than their own opinion; they also have the word of God himself, for God himself has revealed himself to them as a good being, in Christ. What does this mean? Only this: that which is for other peoples (pagans) an *imagined* being, existing only in thought and therefore dubitable, is for Christians a *sensual*, and therefore a certain, being.[12]

If God is for man, he must also be for the senses of man. How can a being which withdraws from before my eyes, my ears, and my touch, be a good being for me? No; that which is against the senses is against man. If God is a spiritual being (that is, a nonsensual being, only existing in thought, only capable of being thought), I must make myself dumb and rob myself of my senses in order to reach this pure being. But a being which deprives me of my body, my senses, and my humanity, is an evil and inhuman being, and, furthermore, an unreliable and uncertain being. For it only becomes certain if I give up the most immediate certainty, the certainty of the senses. But a being whose certainty contradicts what I recognize as the most certain thing of all, a being whose existence rests solely on the apex of thought devoid of sense and therefore is always at the mercy of doubt, is a being which causes man only torment and pain. Only a

[12] [Editor's note: The emphasis in this and the next paragraph on "sensual existence" is a typical expression of what Feuerbach called his philosophic principle of "sensualism"; that is, the priority of the sentient individual in all philosophical discussions. See, for a very brief discussion, the Introduction and, for an extensive treatment, Feuerbach's *Philosophy of the Future,* now available in English.]

sensual being favors and satisfies man and can be a
beneficent being; for only a sensual being is an in-
controvertible and a certain being. And without certainty there is no beneficence. Even the certainty of
the most terrifying object is terrifying only insofar as
it is not an immediate and sensual certainty, but merely
a certainty for the imagination. Imagination is the ape
of actuality; but the more it wants to attain to actuality, the more it misses it. Everything which is immeasurable and limitless for the imaginaton and fancy
has its set bound and measure in actuality. The greatest
and most terrifying evil for the imagination—death—is
precisely the certain, perceptible end of all terror and
evil. Of course, the struggle with death is terrifying,
but even there death is still not an immediate, sensual
certainty—the moment of sensual certainty is also the
moment of expiation and deliverance. Follow your
senses, but do not interrupt them by arbitrary imagin-
ings; let them play out their theme to the end, and
you will find—if only at the end—satisfaction. What
gushing springs are to the body the senses are to the
head and the mind. The senses have curative power;
the senses purify and liberate head and heart. Change
whatever oppresses and alarms you, charms and de-
files you, from an object of the imagination or of
thought into an object of the senses; do this, and you
will certainly become free. Imagination obscures, but
the senses disillusion. Imagination makes one troubled,
fainthearted, misanthropic; but perception makes one
lighthearted, courageous, philanthropic. Crime arises

from the imagination of a deed, but from sensual certainty of a deed comes conscience. Of course, the senses also kindle the fire of lust; but their fire is a vivifying, beneficent fire, while imagination or pure thought is a "consuming fire" like "the divine majesty," which is only an imagined thought, and believed being, but is not an actual or a sensual being.

The fundamental proposition of Christianity— "God has revealed Himself to man; that is, became man (for the Incarnation of God was indeed the Revelation of God)"—has no other meaning but that in Christianity God has become a sensual being instead of a being in thought. A sensual being comes not from my head, but it comes to me from without. It is given to me; my senses have revealed it to me. It is no product of human reason, as is the God of the philosophers, but neither is it a product of human hands, as is the Jupiter of Phidias. It is an independent being, which is consequently given to me not through me but through itself. I only see objects which cause themselves to be seen. A sensual being is a being which offers itself to us; in face of a sensual being I am only passive. It is not an object of activity, but simply an object of observation. What I see is not what I have deserved because of any activity of mine; it is a gift, a fortunate occurrence, for me. Revelation presents what would never have come to a person's mind; but only the senses present to a person what surpasses all his expectations and notions, that to which he would never have attained alone. In short, everything which is asserted of the Revelation of God is true only of sensuality. The essence of Revelation is the essence of sensuality in distinction to human autonomous activity, whether this be moral activity, or artistic activity, or philosophical activity, or religious and ritual activity, such as that of the Jews and Papists.

Christ is thus the humanness of God as a man—the divine being (i.e., the being good to us, for God—not nature—is the unlimitedly, exclusively, unmixedly good being) as an infallible and certain (that is, sensual) being. And sensuality is by no means merely a matter of form, appearance, or accoutrement, a matter of the popular expression of a thought in itself unpopular; it is a thing, a being in itself. For a universally, and consequently a truly, good being is, as we have indicated, necessarily a being which operates for the senses. A being which operates for the senses is also a being which operates for the understanding, but the reverse is not necessarily true—namely, that what is conceived of as a being by the understanding must also be perceptible by the senses. In a word, what is good for the senses is good for the entire man, but only what is good for the entire man is also in itself a thoroughly perfect good.

Now let Luther himself speak and testify that the revelation of God in Christ has no other meaning than that which has been expressed.

Even the heathens have experienced it and have had to testify that one cannot with certainty reach God

through thought or rational investigation. Therefore, think this saying over carefully—"How sayest
thou then, Shew us the Father? (John 14:8, 9)."
Rather, do not flirt with that which is merely the
thought; hear and stick with the "Whoever sees
Me, also sees the Father" (45:526).

From a God Who is not revealed, I wish to become
a revealed God, and yet I wish to remain the same
God. I wish to become a Man or to send My Son;
and thus I want to fulfill your desire and satisfy
what you want to know—whether you are elected
(predestined to blessedness) or not. Behold, this is
My Son, Whom you shall listen to; behold Him—
and you will certainly apprehend Me. For He that
hath seen Me, says Christ (John 14), hath seen the
Father. No one has ever seen God. And yet God
has revealed Himself to us out of great mercy (i.e.,
goodness and love). He has presented us with a
visible exact image, and has said, "Behold, you have
My Son; whoever hears Him and will be baptized is
inscribed in the book of life. This I reveal to you
through My Son, Whom you can touch with your
hands and see with your eyes."

And He proves and confirms this not with spiritual
arguments, but with tangible arguments and signs.
For I do indeed see the water (in baptism), I see the
bread and wine (in the Last Supper), I see the
servant of the Word, all of which is bodily, in

which bodily figures or images He reveals Himself.
Indeed, He has established all this because He
wished to make you quite certain and take from
your heart the great fault and error of doubt, so
that you would not only believe in your heart, but
also might see with bodily eyes and touch with
your hands. Why then do you overthrow all this
and complain that you cannot know whether you
have been elected for blessedness (*43*:459, 462,
460)?

Therefore Peter says, "We have announced and
made known to you the Christ, that He is a Lord
and rules over all things, etc. This we have not in-
vented ourselves, but we have seen and heard it
through God's revelation" (*14*:27).

He lived among us. He did not appear as did the
Angel Gabriel, for angels do not live visibly among
people. Rather, He dwelt with us (says the Evan-
gelist) in His human nature, which in His Incarnation was united indissolubly with the divine nature;
He ate, drank, became angry, prayed, became sad,
cried, etc., with us.

He was no phantom, but a veritable Man.

The Manichaean heretics were disturbed that the
Son of God should become a man. It is frightening
to hear that they claim that Christ neither ate nor

drank anything, that the Jews did not indeed crucify the true Christ, but a phantom.

Thus it is the noblest treasure and highest comfort we Christians have that the Word, the true, natural Son of God became Man, Who had flesh and blood just as any other man, and became Man for our sake, so that we might come to great glory, so that our flesh and blood, skin and hair, hands and feet, stomach and back may sit in heaven above, near God. That we might boldly defy the Devil and whatever else fights with us. For thus we are certain that these (we) belong in heaven and are the heirs of the kingdom of heaven (46:631).

And we saw His glory. What is this? He has not only shown by His manner that He is a true man, but also, through His glory and power, let it be seen that He is God. His doctrines, preachings, miracles, and wondrous deeds have shown this. Thus, just as God created heaven and earth by His word (i.e., through Him), even so He has directed and done what He wished by speaking only one word, such as "Maid, stand up," or "Youth, stand up," "Lazarus, come out." To the palsied man, "Stand up, be rid of your illness," and to the leper, "Be purified." Also, He fed with five loaves of bread and two fishes five thousand people, so that they who saw this sign said, "This is truly the Prophet who is to come into the world." Also when a great tempest arose in the sea and the Lord threatened the sea and it was still, those who were in the ship were amazed and said, "Who is this man whom the wind and the sea obey?" Also, He commanded the devils and they had to leave. He could do all this through a single word (46:634–635).[13]

But what are miracles, then? Visible, evident proofs of omnipotent and unhampered goodness and mercy, bound by no limitations of nature; evident and tangible "good deeds," benefits. But what are benefits? Gratifications of human needs, fulfillments of human wishes. No benefit can be rendered to a person who needs nothing, desires nothing, and wishes for nothing. The wish of the unwell person is health, the wish of the hungry person is food, and so forth. To be good a person must give me what I do not have, but want to have or at least would like to have; provided, of course, that this object is not in itself evil, bad, or unjust. The miracles of Christ or God are distinguished from the miracles of the evil, God-opposed being, the Devil, precisely in that the Devil's miracles (which, simply because they are the Devil's, are limited in power and only superficial) operate for man's detriment and destruction, whereas God's operate for His temporal and eternal well-being.[14] (See,

[13] "The Gospels say nothing of the divinity of Christ." This may be true, but what they do not say in words they say in deeds. Words are prosaic, deeds poetic.

[14] [Editor's note: Reading *Wohl*, as in the 1844 edition, instead of *Wahl*. The sense and the gender of the article also support the change.]

in regard to this, L.; for example, Volume 45, 529–530.)

But as is the deed, so is the doer. Beneficence pre-supposes a beneficent being; and a beneficent, good being is precisely what God is by his very nature. Thus Christ is the invisible essence of God made into a visible and sensually perceptible being.

> For if He (God) had pleasure in being angry, in damning, in punishing and plaguing, He would not forgive sin through Christ and remove the punishments of the palsied man, the leper, and others. Also, if He had pleasure in death, He would not reawaken and revivify the dead. Thus we are certain not only concerning the article that Christ is a true God along with the Father, but also that He is a merciful God and Savior, and that we can apprehend in all the works of the Lord Christ ("Which you see before your eyes"), the heart and will of the Father, to our right blessed confidence (45:527–528).

What you think God is, you see in Christ; what God is in the form of thought, Christ is in actuality. If you do not recognize Christ as God, it is only because of the distinction which exists between a being as it is thought to be and the same being as it actually is; for the being which is thought is a general being, whereas the actual or sensual being is individual. But this distinction (or rather contradiction) apart, you have in Christ—before your eyes—exactly what you think of as God (at least in the Christian sense). The distinction between God and Christ is that between what is thought or conceived and what is said. To thought, the word is always too narrow, just as man is to your God. Thought does not want to be encroached upon by the word. It always has something in reserve which it has wished to leave unsaid; it imagines itself infinitely superior to the word, and therefore does not want to let itself be limited by the word. This thought, however, is only derived from the fact that what I think of or conceive still lies in my power, whereas what I express is outside the reach of my power; it is only derived from the fact that thought or an idea, because dependent on me, are mutable, while the word, because already independent of me, is immutable. For this reason, man becomes frightened at his own expressed words as at a strange power or as at the power of immutable necessity, and shyly pulls himself back under the bulwark of his inexpressible thought. Still, the distinction between word and thought is not one of essence, but only one of condition; it is only the distinction which in nature subsists between the gaseous or fluid state and the solid state. There is the same content, the same essence, in what I think and what I say (if I say it properly and suitably), but in thought it is in the unrestrained—gaseous or liquid—state, while in word it is in the solid state. The same thing is true of God and Christ. The God in your head is gas and wind; the God in Christ is a fixed and solid body.

How can the large encompassing being enter into the small body of man? As gas it cannot, of course, for gas is not tangible and takes in a larger space than the solid body. In order to become a solid body, it must cease being a gas. In order to speak, I must cease merely thinking; in the same manner, to become a sensual and comprehensible being, I must cease being a nonsensual one. Gas cannot at the same time be a solid body; what is thought cannot at the same time be what is said. For if it is something said, it is no longer something merely thought; and if it is something thought, it is no longer something said; one excludes the other. And, according to this same way of thinking, you are quite correct when you say, "If it is God, it is not man, and vice versa." But when God becomes a man, he ceases being what he is in your thoughts; namely, God, or an invisible, incomprehensible, unlimited, inhuman, nonobjective being. Of course, if you do not bring the God in your mind out of yourself, a crucified God is just as laughable a contradiction[15] as a thought corporeally punished with torture. For only what I say, what I reveal of myself,

[15] Faith—that is, the Christian religion—never gets out of this contradiction. For Christ is supposed to be at the same time man and God; that is, word and thought-being, or solid body and heavenly gas. But in this essay we turn away from this contradiction, as from all the other heinous contradictions of Christianity, which are treated in the second part of *The Essence of Christianity*.

[Editor's note: See the Introduction. What Feuerbach means, briefly, is that in the second part of *The Essence of Christianity* he had discussed the "false" side of religion; that is, the fact that Christianity separates human characteristics from man and honors them in a superhuman and supernatural being.]

or what I place outside myself can be an object of criminal law, but not what I think or what I conceive. The question "How can God be crucified?" is thus the same as the question "How can thought or ideas be corporeally punished?" And the answer is, "By making the thought into a being perceptible and objective to others besides yourself; that is, by making it into a sensual being." Pure thought, of course, is unattainable and irrefutable, exalted above all attacks and limitations, a divine untouchable majesty. But the thought which glides down the slippery tongue out of the mighty fortress of the head—the thought which degrades and lowers itself in words—takes all the curse and hardship of human life upon itself. Thus, also, the God in our head, that God who is a being only thought and internal (that is to say, is only a thought) cannot, of course, be an object of scorn and laughter; whereas the God in Christ (that is, the expressed God) can be such an object. For to express oneself means to betray oneself, to externalize oneself, and to surrender oneself. And yet there is nothing expressed in Christ which is not thought in God. The only distinction is that what is still uncertain in God (because it is only thought) is indubitably certain in Christ; for the word is the certainty of the thought. Pure thought is unstable and inconstant; it is scarcely with us and it is gone again. But thought captured in words is fixed—a word is steady, solid, and certain. But Christ is the Word of God—that is, precisely, as ex-

pressed, the visible, sensual, and hence indubitable and
certain God.

"What!" I hear someone mention despite the proofs
I have already developed, "A sensual and visible being
is the object of the Christian revelation and of the
Christian faith? Is it not expressly stated, 'Faith is
turned toward the invisible—faith is not of things
seen, but of those not seen' " (Heb. 11:1) (III, 123).
Does not Luther say that Christ is not an object of the
senses in order that he may be an object of faith?[16] Is
it not stated expressly here that the invisible is the
object of revelation—for what else is the object of
faith but the word of God? In any case, God, or
Christ, is now no object of the senses to us, but he
once was and will be again. Now only his word is in
our ears, but once his being was before our eyes.
Abraham is the prototype of faith. Abraham believed
the promise of God. But what was the object of this
promise, this belief? A son—a being now invisible, but
visible in the future.

> Faith has such acute eyes that it can see in the dark
> where there is apparently nothing; it sees where
> nothing is to be seen, feels when there is nothing to
> be felt. Thus we also believe of the Lord Christ that
> He sits up there at the right hand of the omnip-
> otent Father and so rules that He has all creatures

[16] See, for example, L.'s *Letters*, edited by de Wette (*Br.* 2:526),
and, in explanation of this, the statement of L.'s cited in *The Essence
of Christianity*, 2nd [German] edition, p. 301.

in His hands and effects everything in us. We do not see this, nor do we feel it; but the heart sees as certainly in faith as if it saw with eyes (24:247).

Faith is the spiritual eye, the eye of the imagination. It sees what it does not see; that is, what it does not have before its eyes at present. Faith does not adhere to that which is present; it sees just as I see a being separated and removed from me by death or space. Faith is separated from the object of its reverence. The wall of this present sensual world is between it and God, but faith breaks through this wall. It is separated, but not separated; it is in spirit where it is not in body. To faith the distant is near, but, for this very reason, the closest thing is the farthest. Faith is nonsensual and countersensual, blind and deaf, for its mind [*Sinn*] is in one place, its senses [*Sinne*] in another. Whoever sees what has departed does not see what is present. But to be separated from a being by the body, and yet to be bound to it by the heart, is a condition of dismemberment and constriction; for my heart violently tears itself loose from the bonds of my senses—a painful dualism. So at some time this dualism is removed; at some time faith changes to observation; at some time God is for the believer what he is now only in himself—a sensual being.

The Kingdom of Christ now on earth is a kingdom of faith, in which He rules through the Word, not in visible public beings, but it is just as when one sees the sun through a cloud.

You are not to see it, but to believe it; not grasp it
with your five senses, but with these shut up (with
the senses closed) yet hear what God's word says to
you—until the hour comes when Christ will make
an end of this and publicly (openly, visibly) present
Himself in His majesty and sovereignty. Then you
will *see* and *feel* what you now *believe* (*36*:*570*).

Christ is the sensual certainty of God's love to man.
He is himself the man-loving God taken as a sensual
object or sensual truth. But the infallibility and re-
liability of this love lie precisely, as said, only in its
humanness; for only a being itself actually human can
love man, at least in a manner satisfactory to, and appropriate to, man. Love from the standpoint of a nonhuman or superhuman,[17] nonsensual, nonsuffering
God or being is an obvious deception; for if humanness falls away, love falls away with it. The meaning
of the redemption and atonement of man with God
through Christ lies, therefore, not in the representation, the atonement, the justification, the bloodshed in
themselves, but only in the love or (what is the same
thing) humanness of Christ or God. The wrath or
hatred of God toward man, silenced and resolved
through the blood of Christ, is the inhuman God
abolished and resolved through man and in man. God
is not God; that is, not an inhuman, nonsensual being.
He is love: he is a man. Through this all the dualism

[17] Of an actually superhuman one, for the superhuman being of
faith is only the superabundantly and superhumanly *human* being.

between God and man is resolved; through this the sins of man are forgiven and man justified.

There are many loves, but none is so ardent and fiery as nuptial love. Such a real nuptial love God has presented us in Christ, in that He has caused Him to become a man for us and united to human nature, so that we might discover and recognize in Him His friendly will toward us. It must indeed be a great, unfathomable, and inexpressible love of God toward us, when the divine nature unites with us and sinks down to our flesh and blood; when God's Son becomes truly one of us with flesh and body and accepts us so completely that He not only wishes to be our Brother, but also our Spouse, and turns to us and gives us as our own all His divine goods, wisdom, justice, life, strength, and force, so that through Him we may participate in the Divine Nature, as Saint Peter says. And as a bride abandons herself with heartfelt confidence to her spouse, and considers the spouse's heart for her own heart, so should you abandon yourself from the depth of your heart to the love of Christ, and have no doubt that He is as much of a mind with you as is your heart (*10* III:415, 416; *22*:336–337).

I may say that I have read no more lovely words spoken of God's Grace in the Scripture than these two words, *chrestotes* (kindness) and *philanthropia* (love toward man), Titus 3, 4, in which Grace is so described that it not only forgives sin, but also dwells among us, goes around with us in a friendly manner, is willing to help and eager to do everything we may desire, as a willing friend from whom one confidently and rightfully expects all good things (*10* I 1:101–102).

"This is My dear Son, in Whom I have pleasure." If I know and am certain that the Man Christ is God's Son and pleases His Father, I am also certain that all the speeches, actions, and sufferings of Christ which happen for me (as He says) must please God in a heartfelt manner. Now, how could God be more effusive and present Himself in a more loving and sweeter manner than in saying that it pleases His heart that His Son Christ speaks with me in so friendly a manner, thinks of me in so heartfelt a manner, and suffers, dies, and does everything for me with such great love. Because Christ, then, lays hold of God's heart with such pleasure—because He is yours with all His speeches and actions and serves you, as He Himself says—thus you certainly also give God the same pleasure and are just as deeply in God's heart as Christ is (*20*:227, 228 f., 230).

"Outside Christ, God takes no pleasure in man," "Only in Christ does God love men," as L. himself says. Why? Because God cannot love man or have pleasure in him if he is not a man in and for himself. Only in Christ—not considered in himself, without and outside Christ—does he forgive men's sins; but forgiveness is an act of love. Why? Because a being which excludes humanness from itself is an inhuman being, and necessarily also condemns the sins of men. To the inhuman legislator, the man who transgresses his commandments stands before his eyes not as a man, but only as a transgressor or a sinner. He therefore mercilessly sentences the man to death with the sinner, without distinguishing the two. To be merciful to the sinner, I must respect the man; I must set up the man as intercessor or mediator between the judge and the sinner. I must warm my cold, peremptory understanding in the blood of man. But how can I do this if I myself am only a bloodless phantom? I, myself, therefore, must above all else be an actual, full, complete man in order to be able to recognize the man in the sinner and to purify and pardon the sinner through the man. Only man can forgive the sins of man. That the man Christ is at the same time God (so that it is said, "Not man, but God alone, can forgive sins and extinguish them") is self-evident; for (other reasons aside) if the man Christ is not God, the being separate from man—the superhuman or inhuman being—remains as the highest and divine being, and sins remain in an unextinguishable and atrocious contradiction with it. Still, it is only as a man that God forgives sin. Only the blood of Christ, as the visible sign of the blood relationship of the divine being with the human being, only this "love blood," as Luther several times calls it, is truly the forgiveness of sins and at the same time the pledge of this forgiveness. For how should an equal condemn an equal; how should blood condemn blood?

> Whoever has grasped this image in his heart—that God's Son became a Man—can see in the Lord Christ nothing evil, but everything good. For I well know that I am not willingly angry with myself, nor do I desire to do harm to myself. But Christ now is just as I am; He is also a true man. How can He, then, intend evil to Himself—that is, with us, who are His flesh and blood (52:44–45)?

No; whoever takes flesh and blood upon himself also takes sin upon himself, for sin comes necessarily from flesh and blood. If he himself hates and rejects sin, he nevertheless lets them fall away for the sake of the being of the sinner; he does not count them. He, of course, sees the sins and errors with his infallible sight, but he does not place the sins before the being (in which case he would not see the forest for the trees), but rather behind the being; that is, in the shadows, not in the light. He, as a being itself human, expounds the sins of men in a human sense—in a good sense.

> God acts as a father toward his son. If someone says, "Look, your son squints," the father says, "He is winking." Even his warts look good to him. Thus does Christ also: "Ah, it is not a sin; it is only weakness in the poor sinner" (45:404).

> But the sin which we do daily, you say, insults and

angers God; how, then, can we be holy? Answer: Mother love is much stronger than the excrement and filth of the child. Thus God's love toward us is much stronger than our filth or impurity. For this reason, even if we are sinners, we do not lose our childhood because of our filth (*Table-Talk*, Eisleben, 1566, 186).

Sin robs man of peace of mind, joy, courage, and self-esteem. It crushes and destroys man—that is, the believer, for whom sin has as a consequence the wrath of God, the loss of grace and eternal blessedness. But the incarnation (that is, humanization) of God is at the same time the "deification of man." Insofar as God is man, man is, at the same time, God. What the consciousness of sin takes from me, Christ (insofar as I am aware of the divine nature of man) returns to me. Indeed, the honor which I obtain through Christ makes me quite insensible to the disgrace which sin inflicts upon me. How can the yelping of the newspapers trouble me when I read my name inscribed in the book of immortality? How can the reproach of my anxious and embarrassed conscience[18] trouble me, when heaven itself re-echoes with my praise because of the distinction shown me in the incarnation of God? How can the snakebite of the Devil on my heel trouble me (*24*:110), when the poison does not pene-

[18] "What can sadden us, except perhaps our sin and bad concience? But Christ has taken these away for us, even if we sin daily" (L.'s *Letters*, edited by de Wette, *Br.* 7:336). See also in the same work the very interesting letter to H. Weller, IV, 188.

trate into my blood and my heart? How can the spot
on my feet caused by the mud of the street trouble
me when my head shines in heaven as a star of great
magnitude? How can the shadow behind my back
trouble me when I have light before my eyes? If the
great Being [*Wesen*] is for me, how can the Monster
[*Unwesen*] be against me?

> When the heart is pure, everything is pure and
> nothing is harmful, although everything external
> might be impure, although the body might be full
> of abscesses, pimples, and leprosy (32:330).

The above-mentioned crude and offensive theological conceptions of representation, justification,
atonement, even of mediation and expiation, only
occur, therefore, because behind the human, sensual
God there still remains the old wrathful God, before
whom men as sinners are nothing, because he does not
look upon sinners as men—there still remains the
"separated," "mere" God; that is, the inhuman nonsensual God. For a human God would himself be the
representative and justifier of man—he would need no
mediator between himself and man. But it is a contradiction that behind the human God the inhuman one
should still continue his existence [*Wesen*] or, rather,
his monstrousness [*Unwesen*]. For with the incarnation of God the inhuman being is removed—as well
and as necessarily removed as is gas when it has become a solid body—and in its place there has stepped
a new being, another being, the human God, the

human Being. If the human God does not step into
the place of the inhuman one—if he is only a middle-
man between the inhuman and the human being—then
the reconciliation between these two beings is only a
superficial, seeming, and even deceitful one. For only
the wrath of God is removed, but not the basis of this
wrath—the being which is angry, and according to its
nature necessarily angry, with man, for it has no
human heart or essence in itself. Its reconciliation with
man is, strictly speaking, only a pretence, only a restraint which it imposes upon itself; for it preserves its
rancor in its feelings, but it does not externalize it because the mediator has tied its hands.

> Now how could the Father be angry with us? In-
> deed, even the Father becomes a Son and, because
> of the Son, is forced to a certain extent (if I may so
> speak) to become a child, to play with us, to caress
> us (*40* III:651).

> This is, then, the real Christ, for He is here the
> Master of our Lord God (XII, 568).

The human God—and through him every single man,
as L. frequently says—is master of the inhuman one;
but the inhuman God remains an independent power,
a person who therefore necessarily wants to make himself of importance and, indeed, all the more in that he
is the person of highest rank. So how could there be a
true, fundamental peace as long as the superhuman or

(what is the same thing) nonhuman being is not completely put aside?

But despite this contradiction (unsolvable within
faith or Christianity)—that faith (in the fear of its
heart and in the limitation of its understanding) keeps
in mind behind the good and human being the evil
and inhuman one—it still, at the same time, makes the
human God the entire, sole, true God.

> Say that you know of no other God—nor do you
> wish to know of one—than the one Who lay in the
> womb of the Virgin Mary and suckled at her
> breast. Where the God Jesus Christ is, there is God
> Himself and the entire Divinity; there one also finds
> God the Father and God the Holy Spirit. Outside
> this God, outside the Lord Christ, there is no God
> anywhere (*40* III: 338 f.).

All the attributes of God are thus transferred to Christ
and, to be sure, as a man—a transfer which for this
very reason removes the existence of a God separate
from Christ, or at least makes it superfluous; just as
contrariwise all attributes of man are transferred to
Christ as a God, in order to make a true man out of
the God in Christ and a true God out of the man in
him, so "that one cannot pray to Him as God if one
does not also pray to Him as a Man (*40* III:709).[19]

[19] Concerning this matter, the so-called *communicatio idiomatum;*
see further, for example, *50:*587–592; *20:*603–606; IV, 13, *54:*90–92. For
the fact that even here no true, genuine unity can be obtained, see
The Essence of Christianity [German edition], p. 513.

Nothing is in God which is not in Christ; Christ is the manifest (i.e., the open, unreserved) God. In Christ, as Luther says (*30* I:186), God has entirely poured himself out; thus he has kept nothing for himself. How, then, can Luther still distinguish from this God, who has given himself and expressed himself to us exactly as he is, a God-in-himself, an incomprehensible and inhuman being, who only "clothes" and "furnishes" himself as a man in order—a good notion!—to insinuate his inhumanity to man under the guise of humanness? He can do this only by contradicting his true meaning and belief. A god who is not for me what he is in himself evokes and deserves doubt and mistrust, not faith and trust; for I do not know whether he is not for himself exactly the opposite of what he is for me—whether he curses me behind my back while he does good things to my face. But only what evokes faith and deserves faith is God.

Faith is blessedness, unbelief is unblessedness; faith is unity,[20] unbelief is discord; faith is certainty, unbelief is doubt. Upon certainty rests the benediction of light; upon doubt rests the curse of night, which is friend to no man. Doubt depends on the play of chance: today this matter upsets my calculations; tomorrow it is another matter which does so. Faith rests

---

[20] Faith is characterized here solely according to its general or true or human meaning, although this is done on the basis of statements by Luther. It is only for this sense of the word "faith" that the attributes of unity, decisiveness, and blessedness are valid. For insofar as faith touches things (or, rather, nonthings) which contradict "the senses, emotion, and reason," faith is the greatest and most unbearable torture which man can impose upon himself.

on the imperturbable ground of necessity: it is impossible that this being deceives and deludes me or that a veracious being should lie. A veracious being cannot be other than veracious; it cannot also be non-veracious. Faith is the root of love; faith and trust evoke love. Doubt is the root of hatred; doubt and mistrust separate man from man. Doubt casts off; trust attracts. Doubt is unfriendly, faith affable. Unbelief is the hell of jealousy, faith the heaven of certain love. Unbelief sacrifices essence to appearance; but faith does not let itself be deceived by any appearance of contrary qualities in the being to which it has given its trust, for faith knows for certain that no being can be the opposite of itself. Unbelief or suspicion trusts its object no farther than it sees, for it gives it credit only for evil; but faith is certain of its object even when separate and far removed from it, for it gives it credit only for good. Faith itself has only good in mind, just as contrariwise unbelief has only evil in mind. "To believe" means precisely "to believe in good." "Not to believe" means "to believe in nothing good." Faith is the conviction that in general the good is not subjected to the bad, but rather the bad to the good. It is the conviction that the truth, even when it stands quite alone and forsaken, still is and can do infinitely more than deception, even when millions of emperors and popes stand by the side of the latter. Faith does not rely, as does unbelief, on the power of the police and tormenting criminal codes; it does not rely on persons ("men"), on associations ("gangs"), on numbers, on masses, on wealth and titles. It relies only on its good and just cause, and is thus certain of victory even in chains. Faith is the happy outlook that the present day is not the last day under the sun, but that tomorrow will follow today and that what is not here today will be here tomorrow. But unbelief breaks off history with the present; it fancies that today is always, that the "Hippocratic countenance" of the present is the permanent and characteristic expression of mankind. Unbelief sacrifices history to the newspaper; it sacrifices the honor of the future—the honor of history—to a momentary victory and an ephemeral honor. But faith rejects the enjoyment and possession of the present in its certainty that the future belongs to it. "Faith," says Luther, "never has to do with past things, but only with future things. For one does not believe in the things which have happened, but only in the promises of God Who will do things" (*8*: 323). Unbelief limits the sphere of man to the narrow circle of his previous experience; but faith is not bound by the limits of the past and present. It believes in the possibility of what until now has been impossible. "To faith nothing is impossible." Unbelief, therefore, is fainthearted, clever (indeed, too clever), conditional, circumstantial, philistine, disconcerted, timorous. Faith is high-minded, unconditional, laconic, resolute, bold, free, and carefree.

But unconcern, freedom, security, conditionality, necessity, immutability, unity, decisiveness, certainty, blessedness, love, friendliness, affability—the attributes

and indices of faith—are also the attributes and indices
of divinity itself. How can you, then, distinguish in
God a God-in-himself and a God for you? It is precisely God himself who removes the validity and possibility of this distinction. Can you ask light whether
or not it is light? Do you not with this very question
remove the very nature of light? Can you ask an
affable being whether it is only affable for you or
whether it is also affable-in-itself? What is a being
which evokes goodness, faith, and trust other than a
being which is for you what it is for itself? Being
good means precisely being and having nothing for
oneself which one is not and has not for others. Can
an open being be at the same time a closed being, a
communicative one at the same time reserved, an object of faith at the same time an object of doubt and
mistrust? But to be God means precisely to be good in
the highest sense; if you remove the good being, you
remove the divine being. But you do this when you
accept, in distinction from the God for you (that is,
the good being), another God-in-himself (that is, a
being not good and consequently not divine). What
is not good is not necessarily evil. But a God who
comes into your head without the attribute of goodness, a God who robs you of the belief in the good as
the true and final (i.e., divine) being, a God who degrades the good into a mere anthropomorphism or
image or appearance—such a God is in actuality no
God but, rather, an evil being. "God in Himself, God
outside Christ," says Luther, "is a terrifying, fearful

God"; but that which instils only fear and terror is an evil being. The God-in-himself, "the Majesty," is distinguished from the essence of the Devil only in imagination or by name, but not in fact or in essence. The "defiance of the Devil" (that is, the evil being inimical to man) is the belief that God is man and man God. "The enemy of man," the Devil, seeks in all possible ways to combat this belief. But God-in-himself also struggles against this belief, for he does not want to see himself—the "bare," pure being—placed in alliance with the mottled, shabby, and dirty essence of man. If the two coincide in their effects, how can they be separated in their nature? The Devil is, of course, supposed to be the inhuman being, while God-in-himself is supposed to be the superhuman being; but superhumanness is only a subterfuge for inhumanity, just as superrationality is only a subterfuge for ir-rationality and supernaturalness only a subterfuge for unnaturalness. It should be noticed in passing, by the way, that God-in-himself is strictly speaking only God as a metaphysical being; that is, as a pure and dispassionate being of thought. L. was an enemy of metaphysics, abstraction, and dispassionateness. "God hates and despises," says L., for example (44:563), "hard apathy." But what men abhor and reject outside religion they put up with in religion.

The true God, the true object of Lutheran (and in general of Christian) faith, is only Christ; this is only because in him there is possible no further distinction between Christ-in-himself and Christ for us, and therefore in him all the conditions of God are fulfilled, all mysteries of the divine nature are resolved, all objections and doubts are taken away, and all bases of mistrust and suspicion are put aside.

> For this reason, one must first of all and above all things try to learn to trust the goodness of God which He has shown us in Christ, His Son, Whom He gave us because of our sins and death. For otherwise there arises a habit and tendency toward mistrust of God, which becomes insuperable (*25*:189).

> The thoughts of His (God's) Majesty (that is, as Luther says a few lines previously, "of God insofar as He is an absolute Being") are very dangerous. For an evil spirit can put himself in the form of majesty; but he can never put himself in the form of the cross (*25*:139).[21]

That is to say: Christ's essence is an evident, clear, translucent essence; Christ is nothing in himself or for himself which he is not for us. His divine essence is our divine essence; his birth as a man is the birth of our salvation; his victory is our victory; in short, everything which is his is ours. What, then, is the resurrection of Christ in itself? Nothing. For it only signifies our resurrection; it is only the sensual certainty of our resurrection and our immortality. What is the

---

[21] Luther, by the way, had emotional states—vexations—when the evil spirit, the spirit of unbelief, Satan, even took the form of Christ. (L.'s *Letters*, edited by de Wette, *Br. 4*:288f).

God-man for himself? Nothing. For the man Christ is only a God so that he may be a God for us, and only a man so that he may be a man for us. What, in general, is God for himself? Nothing. For God is only God for others; he exists only for that which is not God. Where there is no need in general, there is also no need for God; and where there is no need for God, there is no God. The "basis" of God lies outside God—in man. God presupposes man. God is "the necessary being"; necessary not himself or in himself, but for others—for those who feel or think him necessary. A God without man is a God without need; but to be without need is to be without a basis; it is trifling, an extravagance, vanity.

> God is not the God of the dead, but of the living— Matt. 22:32. God is not the God of the one who in himself is nothing; *nullus* (no one) and *nemo* (nobody) do not pray to God, and God does not rule over them. If Abraham has a God, it follows necessarily that God and Abraham must both live, for these two stand and fall with one another, since God has nothing to do with the dead (43:479).

That is to say: "No man, no God." God is essentially somebody's God. But this "somebody" is, for us, man. God is essentially a lord, but there is no lord without a servant.

"It is necessary for a true God to have His own people" (*10* I 1:266 f.). God is essentially a father,

but there is no father without a child. "There is no
deity without a created object" (26:606).

God is nothing in himself. But how does faith express this, since it presupposes the existence of a God
independent of man? Through grace, favor, mercy,
and goodness; in a single word, "God's love." The dependence of an independent being—the "being-noth-
ing-for-itself" of a being which yet is for itself or is
conceived of as being for itself—is love. To love means
to be able to be and to wish to be nothing for oneself;
it means to place one's essence outside oneself. The
sentence "God is love" (i.e., love is the essence of
God) thus says nothing more than that "God is nothing in himself." But this essence of God—to be
nothing in himself—is only manifest, actual, and pal-
pable in Christ; and only Christ is the true and essential
object of faith. The essence of faith is hence only the
certainty—the imperturbable, indubitable certainty—
that God's essence is love for man, and that love for
man is the supreme being. Faith

> has no tribunal but pure grace, favor, kindness,
> mercy. It must have its source in, and flow from,
> the blood, wounds, and scars of Christ, in which
> you see that God is so gracious to you that He even
> gives His son for you (6:215 and 216).

> Faith could be nothing even though it believed that
> Christ was omnipotent and could do and know all
> things. For only that is a living faith which does not

doubt that God is also *good* and with a merciful will will do what we ask.

Faith toward Christ doesn't at all imagine Him except as the mere grace and goodness of Christ (*17* II:73–74).

Every time Scripture mentions faith, it means faith which builds upon pure Grace ("goodness, mercy, *misericordia*") [*Apologia Confessionis Augustana*, Art. IV (II)].

If our hearts are in affliction, anxiety, and distress, they only believe, perceive, and feel that God is angry with us and pays no attention to us and is inimical to us. Thus, faith ought to hold the contrary view; namely, that there is no anger, no hatred, no punishment, no guilt in God (*40* III: 370).

Let it be firmly accepted that faith in God's favor is certain; for faith is only a constant, indubitable, unwavering confidence in Divine Grace (*10* I 2:139).

Just as God is, through love, the One who gives, so we are, through faith, the ones who receive. Thus this Treasure (Christ) is given by God through love and accepted and received by us through faith; that is, when we believe, as we have heard here, that God is merciful and gracious and shows such mercy and love to us that He causes His own Son to become a man and throws all our sins upon Him (*52*: 332).

To believe and to love—or to receive benefit from God and to show benefit to one's neighbor; all Scripture puts these forth and one cannot be without the other (*10* I 1:99).

Faith receives the good works of Christ; love does good works to its neighbor (*10* I 2:167).

The distinction between Lutheranism and Catholicism is merely the fact that in the former God's love is certain, in the latter it is uncertain and doubtful. (See, in regard to this: *18*:633; *33*:427 and 429; *45*:660 f.) But certainty is the essence of goodness and love; doubt removes love. The God of Catholicism is thus in fact not only a God of doubtful goodness, but also actually an unmerciful, wrathful, inhuman God. For the Catholic wishes to reconcile God to himself through works, sacrifices, self-imposed suffering; he wishes to make amends to God. But just as faith presupposes being, works presuppose nonbeing. God is good to man—this is a matter of faith. God is to be good to man—this is a matter of works and of sacrifice; but what is to be is not now. Faith is quite satisfied with God, and thus has time and place for works useful to man; but the wrath of God does not allow the works-performer any rest or any time for such useful works. Endless wrath on the part of God requires endless sacrifices on the part of men. (See, in this re-

gard, for example: XVIII, 160.) In short, God is for
the believer only a being for man—a being which thus
gives man to man and leads man back to himself; for
the performer of works, God is a being for himself, a
being other than human—a being which thus separates
man from himself and takes man from man. Catholicism, of course, leaves man the power of goodness, will,
and freedom; thus far it appears human. But it leaves
man this power so that he can exist and operate against
himself—so that he can sacrifice himself, torture himself, enchain himself through voluntary statutes—and
through this being-against-himself win God for himself. I can win over a being only with something
which agrees with its essence; I can thus dispose God
in my favor (since he is not for me, but rather against
me) only by being against myself and being evil to
myself. "Papism" or Catholicism is only human in
order to be able to be inhuman, just as, on the other
hand, Lutheranism is only inhuman in order to be able
to be human. In Catholicism, we are only men in
order not to be men; in Protestantism, on the contrary, we are not men in the face of God (before God
we are "miserable carcasses, clods") only in order to
be able to be men in life. We concede everything to
God in faith in order to be able to concede everything
to man in life. In faith we have only to do with God;
but therefore in life we have only to do with men.

Behold, Paul has clearly declared that a Christian
life consists of directing all works for the good of

one's neighbor, while each person has enough for himself in his faith; and all other works and life are superfluous to his serving his neighbor out of voluntary love (7:35).

Thus one being—God—is the object of faith; another—man—is the object of love, that is, of practical activity and of life.

But is this actually the case? No. The object of faith is, as we have seen, love; the supreme article of faith—the only decisive one, the one which encompasses everything—is the proposition "God is love." But love for whom? After all, love in itself and without an object is a chimera. The answer is, "love for man." So, in truth, man is the object of faith also. Philanthropy—love of man—is also the mystery of faith. It is distinguished from love only in that another man is the object of love, whereas I myself am the object of faith. In love I love; in faith I am loved. But loving humbles me, for in this case I subordinate and subjugate myself to another being; being loved exalts me. What I lose in love, I receive again manyfold in being loved. The awareness of being loved is self-awareness, self-esteem; and the higher the being by whom I know myself loved, so much higher is my self-esteem. To know oneself loved by the supreme being is therefore the expression of the highest—indeed, divine—self-esteem. So the distinction between faith and love consists only of the fact that in faith man is a heavenly, divine, infinite being, but in love he

is an earthly, finite, human being. "Through faith,"
says Luther, "man becomes God"; "In faith we are
gods, but in love we are men."[22] For in love I am a
relative being, of use to another person—I am only a
means; but in faith I am an absolute being, an end in
myself. In love I deify another being; but in being
loved I am the deified being. Whoever loves me calls
to me, "Love yourself, for I love you; I only show
you and make clear to you what you are and must do.
My love justifies and, indeed, obligates you to love
yourself." Being loved is the law of self-love. The
object of love is thus philanthropy—real, "profane,"
yes, profane philanthropy—foot-trodden daily, thousands and thousands of times. But the object of faith
is the inviolable holiness of self-love. Love is the heart
which beats for others, but faith is the heart which
only beats for itself. Love makes one unhappy, for it
is feeling and caring for others; but "happy is faith,"
happy the feeling that I am loved, happy self-esteem,
for here everything besides me disappears.

> Faith leads people from people (that is, away from
> men) to God. Thus it means to go out of the eyes
> of people, where one neither sees nor feels anyone
> but God (*12*:683);

that is to say, oneself. Over love stands faith; that is,
over the love of others stands love of oneself.

---

[22] In love also, Luther says somewhere else, man is God; but in love
he is the God of others (he is for them what Christ is for us—a bene-
factor, helper, savior), while in faith he is God for himself. In love I
thus have no part of my divinity—rather, I externalize it; but in faith
I am in full enjoyment of it.

But if one wishes to speak and teach properly of faith, it far oversteps love. For let one only see what faith is concerned with and has to do with; namely, it fights only for God against the Devil, who ceaselessly plagues and tortures us. But such a battle does not take place over minor matters; it concerns death, eternal life, sin, the law which obligates us, Grace, through which our sins are forgiven. If one compares with these weighty matters love, which has to do with minor matters, such as serving people, helping them with advice and deeds, consoling them, who would not see that faith is much higher than love and is to be willingly preferred to it? For how can you even compare God with men? How can you even compare helping and advising a man with that which helps us overcome eternal death (*40* III: 368)?

We are imperfect and weak in our love to others, but strong and insuperable and perfect in our self-love. Love bears all the crimes of humanity with it; but faith—self-love—bears all the perfections of divinity. Love is weak, yielding, patient, suffering, needful, dependent; but faith is far and above everything else haughty, selfish, lordly, intolerant, as is God.

Nothing makes God suffer; nothing weakens Him. For He is immutable. Faith must also be so (*40* I: 182).

As I have often said, faith makes us lords, while

love makes us slaves. Indeed, through faith we become gods. But through love we become as the
poorest person. Through faith we need nothing and
enjoy all things; through love we serve every man
(*17* II:74; see also *8*:355; XI, 516).

Love should never curse, but always bless. Faith has
power and should curse. For faith makes people the
children of God and stands in God's place; but love
makes people the servants of man and stands in a
servant's place (*17* II:53).

First faith, then love. "Love follows faith," but the
first thing is self-love; the second is love of one's
neighbor. This order of progression has a good and
proper sense as well as a bad, egoistic one. For how
will I make others happy if I myself am unhappy;
how will I satisfy others if the worm of dissatisfaction
gnaws at me? How, in general, will I do good to
others if I have nothing good in myself? I must, therefore, first care for myself before I can care for others;
I must first possess before I can share; I must first
know before I can teach. In general, I must make myself an end before I can make myself a means for
others. In short, the object of love (love of one's
neighbor) is the welfare of others, but the object of
faith is my own welfare and blessedness.

God—the object of Christian faith—is nothing but
the satisfied urge toward happiness, the satisfied self-
love of the Christian man.[23] What you desire and wish

---

[23] [Editor's note: In this paragraph, again, Feuerbach foreshadows,

for is fulfilled, attained, actualized in God. But what is your wish and your desire? Freedom from all evils, freedom from sin (because it is the greatest and, besides, the closest evil), freedom from the irresistible power and necessity of sensual drives, freedom from the oppression of matter (which binds you with the chains of gravity to the soil of the earth), freedom from death, freedom, in general, from the limitations of nature—in one word, blessedness. But this blessedness is desired not as a mere unconsoling thought or as a blind hope; that is, it is not desired as an attribute which will come to you only when you are blessed but which has no basis at the present time. God is this blessedness *as an actual being.* "God is blessed, but he does not want," as Luther says (XVII, 407), "to be blessed for himself alone." No. His blessedness is only the assurance, the certainty, the existence of our own blessedness. God is what he is for us—blessed so that we may be blessed. If blessedness is to be no mere dream or empty wish, it must be a being and, to be sure, the supreme being—God. For if the blessed being falls short of other beings, it gives in to these and cannot resist whatever fights against blessedness. Only the supreme being, exalted above all things, can fulfill and satisfy the supreme wish—that wish which is indifferent to all else. God is the blessed being because blessedness is the supreme thought and the supreme essence of man (or at least of the Christian be-

---

even as to vocabulary, the position taken in his later works, such as the *Theogonie.* See the Introduction.]

liever).[24] The basis of the necessity of the blessed being is the [human] desire to be blessed, the urge toward happiness; and, to be sure, the unlimited supernatural urge toward happiness, unlimited in the sense of being separated from all definite matter and all definite objects of sensuality. Thus, just as the belief "Christ has arisen" actually means (according to Luther and according to the object itself) the belief and certainty that "I shall arise," and just as the belief "Christ is the redeemer from sin and its punishment" actually means the certainty that "I am redeemed from sin and death," so also the belief in blessedness or in divinity in general (which is the same thing) actually means the certainty of my own blessedness and divinity.

Wherever Scripture treats of works and commandments of the first table (i.e., of God), there is uncovered and indicated the resurrection of the dead. Thus God's service—faith and prayers—decrees in itself the articles of the Resurrection and eternal life (*40* III:493 and 495).

For in them the doctrine of faith and resurrection of the dead is included, since God says, "I, the almighty Creator of Heaven and Earth, am thy

[24] Not of all men or of man in general? No. The desire for blessedness (of course, in the rapturous sense in which this word is taken here) is a product of Christianity. Of course, man always strives to free himself from all disagreeableness and from all restraint upon his self-esteem and love of life; but this striving is always concerned with definite, actual objects and with definite human ends.

God." This is as much as to say, "Thou shouldst live in the life in which I also live" (*43*:221).

The Gospel of the Resurrection of Christ—this is the chief article of our faith (*12*:268).

When one denies the future life, one takes God away completely (*43*:363).

For if there were no other life than this temporal bodily life, what would we need Christ for? But Moses indicates that after this life there is another life, because he in his time of need prays to the God Who is outside this world and invisible. From this it follows that the grace and life we ask of Him are also invisible and belong to another life, which belongs to us and not to the oxen. For God does not care for oxen, as Saint Paul says (*40* III:578).

If you believe, as do Pope, Cardinals, and Bishops, that after this life there is no other life, I would not give a fig for your God (*52*:83).

If we may not await or hope for the Resurrection, there is no faith and no God (*44*:385).

This is the principal article of the entire Christian doctrine—namely, how we become blessed. All theological disputations should see to and be directed at this point; all the Prophets have been most concerned with it. For if this article of the blessed-ness of our souls is held and maintained with a certain and solid faith, the other articles all come and follow easily [Feuerbach reads *gemächlich* for *gemehlich*] thereafter, such as that of the Trinity. Also, God has declared no article to us as openly and clearly as this one; namely, that we become blessed only through Christ. The others are indeed very important, but this one is the most important (*Table-Talk*, 194).

It is (says Saint Peter) through the power of faith that we participate in and are in company or community with the Divine Nature. But what is God's Nature? It is eternal truth, justice, wisdom, eternal life, peace, joy and pleasure, and whatever we can call good. But whoever participates in God's nature is benefited by living eternally and having eternal peace, pleasure and joy, and is perfect, pure, just, and omnipotent against Devil, sin, and death. Whoever wishes to subjugate a Christian must subjugate God (*14*:19).

You are just as much a king as Christ is a King if you believe in Him. He is a King over all kings, Who has power over all things and at Whose feet everything must lie. Just as He is a Lord, I am also a lord, for what He has I also have (*12*:317).

To believe is but to change the "There is a God and a Christ" into the "*I am* a God and a Christ."[25] The

[25] [Editor's note: Reading *Christus* for *Christ* in the second phrase although the 1844 edition agrees with that of 1846. The parallelism is more characteristically Feuerbachian this way, and the sense is better.]

mere belief "There is a God" or "God is God" is a moribund, vain, and empty belief. I only believe if I believe that God is my God. But if God is mine, then all divine possessions are my property; that is, all God's attributes are my attributes. To believe is to make God a man and man a God. The avowed object of faith is only a pretext, a means, an image, a sign, a fable; I myself am the doctrine, the meaning, the end, the content of it. God is the food of man—Luther even compares Christ with a "roast, larded capon"—but the purpose of food is only that I may eat it. What is a roast in itself? To believe is to eat, but in eating I abolish the object in question and I change its attributes into my attributes, flesh and blood. Thus the bones of animals become red by the use of madder.

Here we have the meaning of the thoughts so often expressed by Luther: "As you believe, so it occurs for you"; "If you believe it, you have it, and if you do not believe it, you do not have it"; "If you believe it, it is, and if you do not believe it, it is not"; "If you believe, for example, that God is good to you, then he is good to you; if you believe the opposite, then he is the opposite." The essence of the object of faith is faith; but I, the believer, am the essence of faith itself. As I am, so is my faith; and as is my faith, so is my God. "As in your heart," says Luther, "so is your God." God is a blank tablet on which there is nothing written but what you yourself have written.

God tells man only what man silently thinks of himself but does not dare to say. What only I say and think about myself is, at least possibly, imagination; but what another person also says about me is the truth.[26] The other person has through his senses what I have only in conception. His eyes tell him whether actually I am or am not what I imagine myself to be. Therefore, if another person confirms what I think, I am certain of it. And the more timid a person is—the less self-awareness and self-confidence he has—the more he must be told and persuaded by others. Telling tells very much; telling makes something of nothing. The creation *ex nihilo* is, actually, the omnipotence of the spoken word. Words "make" people even more than clothes. Very many who are nothing think they are something and actually become something only because others say they are something. Others, on the contrary, who have enough material, ability, and capacity, believe themselves nothing and actually become nothing in consequence of this depressing belief, until a voice from outside calls out to them that they are something. But many have, through their deeds, already proved to the entire world that they are something and yet are at the same time nothing for other people until still others tell these other people that they are something. One person believes and repeats it to another, and so one is sent from Pontius to Pilate until one finally comes to a man who has the courage

---

[26] [Editor's note: The discussion at this point of the You (or Thou) as the corroborator of the I or ego is an important characteristic of Feuerbach's philosophy; see *Grundsätze der Philosophie der Zukunft*. Twentieth-century existentialist philosophers such as Martin Buber recognize a debt to Feuerbach in this connection.]

and spirit to say something not after, but before, others. Faith derives from hearing; faith is based on the spoken word. Credulous people thus believe everything that is told them, and, to be sure, for no other reason than that it is told them.

But whence this power of the word spoken by another man, if it says exactly what I myself say or at least *can* say? Merely from the fact that it is the word of a being existing outside me—another being, an objective being. But the service performed for me in actual life by another man is performed for me in religion by God. In life the You is the God of the I; in faith God is a man's You. God is the essence of man, but as a being separate from him—as an objective being. God is the father of man. The father is what the child is not. He is for the child what the child cannot be for itself. The child is dependent, unfree, incapable of caring for and protecting itself; but what it is not in itself, it is through its father—free and independent. The child does not have to beg, does not depend on the will of strangers, and is not nakedly placed against the attacks of hostile powers; it is cared for and sheltered. With the help of its father it goes through all dangers just as confidently as the man who depends only upon his own power and judgment. The power of the father is the child's power. The child cannot attain for itself what it wishes; but by means of its father it is master and lord of the things it wants. The child does not feel dependent upon its father. I feel dependent only upon a despotic being, not upon one

who loves me; I feel dependent only when I am un-
willingly dependent, in opposition to my impulse toward freedom. But the child is joyfully a child; it has
in its father its self-esteem (children are proud of their
parents), and it has the feeling that its father is not a
being for itself, but rather a being for it, the child.[27]
The father has only physical power; but the true
power, the one which determines and rules the physical ability to act, the child has in its hands—namely,
the father's heart. As a man, as a being perfect in
power and understanding, the father stands over the
child, but only to stand under the child as father—that
is, in his heart. The father is only lord of the child in
order to be able to be the servant of its needs and
wishes. The heart is the ruler of the earthly, as of the
heavenly, father. But where, then, does the real distinction between father and child lie? Only in this: in
the father there is present as an object what in the
child is only a propensity; in the father there is actuality, whereas in the child there is only a goal for
future development; in the father there is something
present which in the child is something future; in the

[27] The religious feeling of dependence is related to God only insofar as he expresses the essence of nature, in opposition to the human
essence. But, as in *The Essence of Christianity*, I was not concerned in
this passage with God as the essence of nature, preferring rather to
leave the treatment of this for a special discussion.

[Editor's note: The "special discussion" of God as the essence of
nature was *The Essence of Religion* of 1845, in which Feuerbach saw
religion as the result of man's feeling of dependence, on nature or on
man. See the Introduction.]

father there is something actual which in the child is a wish and a striving. The child determines itself according to the father; the father is its model and its ideal. In short, the child has in its father what it will possess as a mature man; except that it has in the father *outside* itself what it will later have *in* itself, and that what later will be in the child as its own nature is now presented in its father as a being separated from the child. The father is and says what the child is to be, can be, and will be. The father is the natural prophet of the child; he is the promise (already fulfilled in him) of the future lying before the child and already hovering before the hope and imagination of the child.

God is that object which holds up before man his own nature, which only calls out to man what he himself [i.e., man] is; not, of course, according to the senses or the body or actuality, but according to his wishes and his desire—namely, a being exalted above all limitations of nature, a being omnipotent, immortal, and divine (that is, blessed, for all divine attributes and all articles of faith ultimately resolve themselves in blessedness). Only that which saves man from all evils, only that which makes him blessed, is God. Christ is called expressly the bearer of bliss [*Seligmacher*]. But what does it mean to say he makes us blessed? It means that he brings about what we wish for, that he fulfills and actualizes our wishes. What, then, is God? The blessedness of man as a fulfilled and actual (that is, objective) being. God is the pledge or the promise of your blessedness; and, to be sure, a promise already confirmed and no longer doubtful. This word [i.e., blessedness] is thus meaningless and spoken in vain—a senseless sound—if you do not believe it, for it concerns only you; it thus only has significance if *you* understand it and apply it and relate it to *yourself*.

Thus God—or the divine being—is simply the being who expresses, promises, and objectifies human (or, rather, Christian) wishes, the focus of which is the wish for blessedness. God is thus nothing but the essence of the human heart—or, rather, emotion—objectified to itself as the supreme, truest, and most actual being.

Take up anything you like; you will find nothing better or more desirable to wish for than to have God Himself, who is Life and an inexhaustible abysmal depth of all good and eternal joy. Now there is no nobler thing on earth than life, and all the world fears nothing so much as death and desires nothing more ardently than life. We are to have this treasure in Him, beyond all measure and ceaselessly (36:599).

What do all men desire more fervently than to be rid of death? Now, this God became a Lord and God so that we may be rid of death and become blessed, which is what all men desire; and His rule is only in making us blessed and being a God to rid us of death (*8:22*).

"All authority," He says in Matt. 28:18, "hath been given unto Me in heaven and on earth." Thus we shall attain what we desire and our heart will not doubt, as the hearts of Turks and Jews must doubt (*40* II:263).

What could or would we desire more ardently, if it were up to us, than to have such a Mediator and Intercessor with God? For how could or should He not hear this Priest, His own beloved Son? How can He refuse or fail to give Him what He asks for? Now, He asks for nothing but our welfare (*41*:193).

God gives us more than we can understand, let alone ask for and desire. Therefore, the great and superabundant salvation far exceeds our requests and desires. For this reason, the Lord Christ has indicated to us how we should make requests and pray; if He had not done this, who would be so bold as to ask such great and excellent things of God (*40* III:373 f.)?

Thus He is as consoling, friendly, loving a Lord as we could ever wish for;

that is, as we could wish for according to our wishes (*37:51*).

Christ has done for you and given you everything
you might seek or desire for yourself, here and in
the beyond; this includes forgiveness of sins, merit
of blessedness, and whatever it may be called. He
comes freely of Himself, out of pure love, so that
He may only do good, be useful and helpful. Behold, now, whether or not He keeps the law of
"Whatever you want people to do for you, do for
them." Is it not true that everyone would wish,
from the bottom of his heart, that someone else as-
sume responsibility for his sin, that someone else
take it up and wipe it out so that it no longer bites
into his conscience, thus helping him away from
death and saving him from hell? What does anyone
desire more deeply than that he may be rid of
death and hell? Who would not like to be without
sin and to have a good, happy conscience before
God? Do we not see that all men strive after this
with prayers, fasting, pilgrimages, the study of
theology, monasticism, and clericalism? What
drives them? It is sin, death, and hell, from which
they would be safe. And if there were a physician
at the end of the world who could help in this
matter, all countries would be laid waste and everyone would run to the physician and would risk
property, body, and soul on the trip. And if Christ
Himself were besieged by death, sin, and hell, as we
are, He also would wish that someone would help
Him out by taking His sin from Him and giving
Him a good conscience. Therefore, because He

would want someone else to help Him in this way, He rushes in and helps others in this way, as the law commands, and takes responsibility for our sin; He goes in against death and overcomes for us sin, death, and hell, so that henceforth all who believe in Him and call upon His name should be just and blessed, without sin and death (*10* I 2:41 and 42 f.).

But each person can only be free of sin and death—blessed—for himself. Just as no one can believe for another (XVIII, 161), so no one can be blessed for another. There can be no sin without something outside me—an object. But for blessedness there need be nothing but myself. One can sin only in human society, but one can be blessed quite alone. Sin ties bonds, but blessedness abolishes all bonds; blessedness takes away all needs. Sin is need, and "need holds all things together," but blessedness is abundance. Sin begets men—all men, according to Christianity, owe their origin to sin ("We have naturally a filthy and sinful conception and birth"); sin thus gives other beings the pleasure of existence. But blessedness is unfruitful; it brings forth and produces nothing out of itself. The blessed, to be sure, form a group, but it is a group based on no necessity or need for one. Of course, I wish blessedness for others, but only because it is the supreme object for me and I presuppose the same sentiment in others. In short, in blessedness I am not related to other beings, but only to myself. Blessedness is indissoluble and inseparable from myself, for it is only my ego itself, freed from all dependency, necessity, obligation, and ties. It is my deified ego. Blessedness is the supreme wish and the supreme essence of Christian (that is, supernatural) self-love; but blessedness is also the final goal—the essential object, or, rather, the supreme being—of the Christian faith. Thus the essence of faith, as distinguished from love and considered according to its ultimate aim, is simply the essence of self-love.

Indeed, faith joyfully sacrifices goods and blood, body and life. But it merely sacrifices transitory welfare and life to eternal welfare and life, perishable goods to imperishable goods, limited and finite joy to infinite and immeasurable and endless joy.

> How precious and noble is this bodily life; and who would give it up for all the kingdoms, gold, and property on earth? But it is less than a moment in comparison with eternal life and goods (XIII, 725).

> I would not give one moment in heaven for the good and joy of all the world, even were it to last for thousands and thousands of years (36:595).

The true believer thus has (naturally, if he gives heed only to the inspirations of faith) no other wish than to die (see, for example, 12:683; 267). That is, he has no other wish than to do away with all worldly and social bonds, all bonds of humanity and love (the object of which is only temporal, but not the eternal, life); and to do away with them bodily, just as he has already done away with them spiritually, for "the spirit is already in heaven through faith" (*12*:267).

COMMENTS UPON SOME REMARKABLE STATEMENTS BY LUTHER

Ludwig Feuerbach (1844)

I

He [Christ] was just such a man as we are. The greatness and consolation of Christ lie in the fact that we recognize Him for such a man as we are and do not wish to flee from Him, nor do we have an aversion to Him, for there is no creature more delightful than a man. The lonely man perceives it clearly; for if he walks at night, it is not so delightful to hear a dog or a horse as it is to hear a man; for a man provides one with more good than if one heard an angel (which would frighten and startle one, as the examples of Scripture indicate frequently). And although at times men are wicked and evil to one another, it is nevertheless the very manner and nature of *man* in Christ that causes us to have recourse to Him in times of vexation and need, as to the One Who can help us (*16*:220 f.).

Do you hear what Christ is? He is an *image of man*—not an image of God, of a being separated from man and opposed to man. Men are at times—indeed, only too often—unfriendly and wicked to one another. But this animosity, this wickedness, is not the true manner and nature of man. No, the true manner and nature of man is that man is good to man; for only he truly means well to himself who means well to others. Hatred is a consuming poison, love a life-giving balm; doing evil makes one evil, doing good makes one good. And you have a model of this true manner and nature of man in Christ. The doctrine of Christ is, reduced to its truth, the doctrine of man. Christ is man generalized; he is what every human individual should be, and (at least according to his general human nature) can be, objectified as an actual man. "Be what Christ is" means: be a *man*.

II

And it is expressly stated that he [St. Stephanus] saw not an angel, not God Himself, but the *man* Christ, which is the most delightful and most perfect nature, and the one most comforting to man. For a man sees another man as dearer than angels and all creatures, especially when in need (*10* I 1:267).

Indeed, the dearest and most comforting nature to man—especially when in need—is his own nature, human nature. For only a human heart has feelings for human suffering; only a being which itself suffers has feelings for the suffering of others. But is human power not infinitely limited? It is indeed; but the limitation of man's power is not at the same time a limitation of his heart, of his love. Even when you can no longer help, you can at least still love. When nature offers you no more assistance, one wellspring never runs dry for you: the wellspring of heartfelt cooperation, of intimate sympathy. And this spring is curative also, even if it is only ethereal. But does religion, does your God, give you other more successful means and cures? Does God help you when you have come to the limits of physical power? Can you with religious dogma concerning consolation awaken the dead, cure the sick, feed the hungry, clothe the naked?

III

It is nonetheless all too natural to be inclined to flee from God and Christ and to trust in men. Indeed, it is immeasurably difficult to learn to trust in God and Christ, which is the course we have praised and which we are obliged to follow (XX, 236).

Human nature is inclined to flee from God to man? Why do you suppress this inclination? Why do you exchange the natural for the unnatural, the easy for the difficult, the nearby for the distant? Is your trust in a being toward whom you feel a natural disinclination not artificial and forced, and hence untrue?

IV

We must turn our face *ad invisibilia gratiae et non apparentis solatii*, and hope for and await them; we must turn our back upon the *visibilibus* (visible things) so that we may become accustomed to leaving them and separating ourselves from them, as St. Paul says. . . . But this is difficult for us who are unaccustomed to it, and the old Adam turns back to the *visibilia*, since he wishes to rest and remain there, which will not do. For *ea quae videntur temporalia sunt* (the visible is the temporal) says St. Paul, and they do not last (*Br. 6*:393).

The new Adam (i.e., Christ) pulls you up to heaven to the invisible things, but the old Adam (i.e., man) pulls you back down to earth to the visible things. Unfortunate Christian, what a dualistic, mutilated being you are! Because the visible is temporal, you do not want to let yourself be chained by it, you do not want to rest your heart upon it? By the same reasoning, because a flower withers in autumn, do you refuse to enjoy looking at it in the spring? Because day does not last forever, do you refuse to take pleasure

in the light of the sun and prefer instead to close your
eyes to the glories of this world and remain in eternal
darkness? You fool! Are you yourself not a temporal
being? Why do you want to run away from what is
in essence like yourself? And what is left to you
when you take away the temporal, the visible? Nothing is left except—Nothing. Only death, fool, is
eternal; life is temporal.

V

If you find that you are weak, do not remain alone,
but . . . take a brother to yourself, and speak with
him of God and the divine will, as it is said: "When
two or three are gathered in my name, I will be
among them." And it is certainly true that one
alone is too weak, as I myself find, when it often
happens that I feel the need of speaking with a small
child (XXII, 529).

What? Religion, God—the personal, living, present-
day God—God, the friend of your soul, your father,
your brother, your one and all, is not sufficient for
you, does not give you sufficient power and strength
to withstand faintheartedness and other temptations
of the devil? You need for support and strength a
human friend as well, a human brother? The need for
human help, for human consolation, is exactly what
you want to overcome by religion, and yet the word
of God is not strong enough to stifle the voice of
human nature, even if this is only the voice of a child?

When you say this do you not confirm that man finds consolation and strength only in *man*? For who is this savior who, when two or three are gathered in his name, is in the midst of them? Do not deceive yourself! It is only the religious *esprit de corps;* it is nothing at all but human society which is in the midst of them and consoles and supports them, not a spirit standing outside this society and independent of it.

VI

But the Scripture also takes the name of God and also applies it to the blessed, the pious and all children of God, the authorities, the princes and judges, and calls them gods. . . . Thus David and the other princes were gods, for they benefited their countries and helped their subjects when they were in need. Therefore, men also prayed to them and showed them divine honor because of their divine works in benefiting and helping the people. . . . Thus preachers, elders, and taskmasters are to be counted as gods by their listeners, children, servants, and students; for they perform acts which pertain originally to God. They indicate the best things to do; they teach and protect; they help and advise. According to man's need they give and do good (*28*:612–613).

"To do good" means "to be God." But what is the most consoling, the dearest being to man, the one which is better to him than any other? *Man.* Why then do you still seek, foolish Christian, a God outside and over man? Is not man as a judge a being over and outside the quarreling parties; is not man as a father a being over and outside his child, a teacher not a being over and outside his student? Do you not find within human life and nature what you believe you must place outside it in a special being? "Yes, the terrestrial, human gods are only the means through which the supreme, celestial God operates." Only means! But why does the omnipotent being which brings about everything need means? And why are the means so infinitely diverse if their effects are not their own but only operations of one and the same being? Why is there a world at all, if its essence and operation is not its own, but the essence and operation of an extra- and superterrestrial being? Is its existence not a mere luxury? Can God not do by himself (i.e., without the world) what he does through the world, insofar as he desires to do so? And if the beings which are good to me—my parents, for example—are only agents of God, how can you expect me to love and honor *them*? Do you thank the servant who brings you a gift in the name of his master?

VII

If you do not want to believe that there is another, a future life, you have enough of a savior in the Emperor, in your superiors, in your father and mother, who will help you with regard to body,

money, and goods. . . . In this temporal life no one
needs God. . . . But when this temporal life is over
and one is about to die, when the conscience cannot
deny its sins before God's court and must therefore
stand in fear and danger of eternal damnation, then
it is the right time for this Savior Jesus to come.
. . . Then if all emperors, kings, princes, fathers,
mothers, physicians, sages, and clever men stood
and wanted to help you, they could not help you
. . . for it is determined that there shall be no
other savior with regard to sins and death, that no
one shall be able to help here . . . but Jesus (*34*
I: 14–17).

Not for life, but only for (or rather, against) death do
we need a God. In fact, death—as the most perceptible
expression of our finitude and dependence upon another being outside us; namely, nature—is the only
ultimate basis of religion. And the abolition of death,
immortality, is the only ultimate goal of religion, at
least of the Christian religion, and the means of this
abolition is God.[28] But why does the Christian need
a supernatural means to conquer death? Because he
begins by assuming an unnatural presupposition, the

---

[28] Insofar as God is nothing but personified blessedness and immortality, he is, of course, an end; but insofar as he is distinguished
from blessedness and immortality, he is the means to these. God is the
provider of blessedness, the savior, the helper, the physician. But the
physician is as physician only the means toward my own cure. The
expression "means" is inappropriate (in contradiction at least to religious conceptions) only insofar as God is thought of as a personal
being. But he is also in fact and in truth nothing but the means by
which man realizes his own blessedness.

presupposition that death is a consequence of sin, a punishment, a destiny brought about by an angry, evil God, to appease whom another God is required—a good and merciful God. But does this means suit its end? No! Against the terror of an unnatural, violent death a supernatural grace can do nothing. Experience shows this, and Luther himself had to undergo this sad experience in his own day. He says, in a letter to N. Amsdorf, that

the fear of death grows greater among the people the more the life in Christ is preached; there is far more fear of death than under popery, when men lived in a secure ignorance concerning the significance of death and the wrath of God. Nevertheless, I hope [he continues] that you will find, as I did, that those who are about to die will die pious and in the faith of Christ. . . . In life they are afraid and weak, but when it comes to death, they suddenly become other men and die with confidence in the Lord. And it is but fair and just that the living should fear but that those who are about to die should find strength in Christ: i.e., that the living feel that they are dying, while the dying feel that they will live (Luther's Letters, *Br.* 8:328).

What a monstrous doctrine it is which, in order to cure an acute evil, changes it to a chronic evil; which, in order to provide for us in the last moments of life a consolation against death, maintains our entire life in terror and fear of death!